MY HOLIDAY IN

NORTH KOREA

THE

FUNNIEST / WORST

PLACE ON EARTH

WENDY E. SIMMONS

RosettaBooks editions are available to the trade through Ingram distribution services, ipage. ingramcontent.com or (844)749-4857. For special orders, catalogues, events, or other information, please write to production@rosettabooks.com.

WENDYSIMMONS.COM | MYHOLIDAYINNORTHKOREA.COM

COVER PHOTO BY WENDY E. SIMMONS

All photos are copyrighted, and exclusive property of Wendy E. Simmons

DESIGN BY ERIN TYLER

Printed in the United States of America. This paper meets the requirements of ANSI/NISO Z39.48-1992 (Permanence of Paper).

ISBN: 978-0-7953-4704-7

EPUB: 978-0-7953-4722-1

MOBI: 978-0-7953-4747-4

LIBRARY OF CONGRESS CONTROL NUMBER: 2015943806

RosettaBooks®

FIRST EDITION

MY HOLIDAY IN NORTH KOREA

" A death-defying adventure, filled with despair and tiny pieces of hope, and beautiful—I wish I was as brave as Wendy."

–JAMES ALTUCHER, BESTSELLING AUTHOR, ENTREPRENEUR, PODCASTER

✧

" Writer and photographer Wendy Simmons shares a personal account of her vacation to one of the most reclusive nations on the planet, North Korea. During her journey she finds herself caught between an international crisis sparked by the release of the Sony Pictures film The Interview and accidentally crashing the 'wedding' of a North Korean bride to be."

–BUZZFEED'S GABRIEL SANCHEZ

✧

" Wendy Simmons gives a glimpse into NoKo in this humorous and en-tertaining book. Through her eyes we see the sometimes absurd, yet always aching existence of a country under the thumb of oppressive rule."

–MYLES KENNEDY, SINGER/SONGWRITER ALTER BRIDGE/SLASH & THE CONSPIRATORS

✧

"My Holiday In North Korea by the very funny Wendy Simmons is a must-read for anyone who wants to lift the veil and spy on the real North Korea. Ms. Simmons happened to be there during the whole debacle surrounding Seth Rogen and James Franco's dumb movie, The Interview, which gives us, the reader, unusual insight into what was actually going on over there during that particularly absurd stand-off. But more than that, it is Ms. Simmons ease at being a traveler to distant and strange lands that gives this book its unusual insight into what people behind a real iron curtain think, and yes, feel."

—MARIA T. LENNON, NOVELIST, SCREENWRITER, AND THE AUTHOR OF *CONFESSIONS OF A SO-CALLED MIDDLE CHILD*, AND *MAKING IT UP AS I GO ALONG* (RANDOM HOUSE)

———————— ✦ ————————

"Wendy Simmons traveled to a place few of us will ever go and found herself in the ultimate Potemkin Village. Her intrepid desire to discover the reality behind the stagecraft escorts the reader through *My Holiday in North Korea* with words and pictures that render this mysterious country both knowable and unknowable, and always fascinating. Simmons' insightful and funny storytelling evocatively captures the deception, corruption, humor and, ultimately, anguished humanity of a bizarre nation. It's a wild trip."

—JON REINER, JAMES BEARD AWARD-WINNING AUTHOR OF *THE MAN WHO COULDN'T EAT*

I have used the names North Korea, Korea, Democratic People's Republic of Korea, DPRK, the Hermit Kingdom, and NoKo—a moniker I believe I may have coined—interchangeably throughout this book.

I have also used the word *Party* (as in, the Workers' Party of Korea, the ruling political party of the DPRK) when I may mean the *Regime*, because I don't know if, or what, the difference may be. Apologies to both.

WENDY E. SIMMONS

WHEN I USED TO READ FAIRY-TALES, I FANCIED THAT KIND OF THING NEVER HAPPENED, AND NOW HERE I AM IN THE MIDDLE OF ONE! THERE OUGHT TO BE A BOOK WRITTEN ABOUT ME, THAT THERE OUGHT! AND WHEN I GROW UP, I'LL WRITE ONE.

LEWIS CARROLL

Alice's Adventures in Wonderland

FOR

Kim Jong-un, the Supreme Leader of NoKo, for being batshit crazy enough to make this book possible. And my handlers, for showing me around.

TABLE OF CONTENTS

NOW, HERE, YOU SEE, IT TAKES ALL THE RUNNING

YOU CAN DO, TO KEEP IN THE SAME PLACE.

LEWIS CARROLL

Through the Looking-Glass

INTRODUCTION

You just know some things are wrong. Being shaken down by a Buddhist monk at a thousand-plus-year-old temple is one of those things.

It was my second-to-last day in NoKo. How anything could still surprise me by that point in my trip, I have no idea. Yet somehow, it did.

Fresh Handler, Local Handler, and I were touring the Pohyonsa Temple (Older Handler had decided to sit this one out and wait with Driver near the car), an eleventh-century temple complex that Local Handler was quick to point out "had suffered extensive damage from American Imperialists during the Korean War."

After we climbed a short set of concrete stairs to the main pagoda and went inside, I put a donation in the wooden box, lit a candle, stood in front of Buddha, and said a silent prayer. I prayed for Fresh Handler's well-being and happiness, hoping against all hope that she would be okay, and I prayed for Older Handler and Driver, since by then I'd grown fond of both of them, too. Then I prayed for all North Korean people, because let's face it, there but for the grace of God go I. It's a stroke of luck, this life we lead: where we're born, how we die. And finally I said a prayer for the Buddhist monk I'd seen standing outside. In a country that "actively discourages" all religion, I couldn't imagine he was having a great time.

When we exited the pagoda, the monk stood waiting. I naively thought to say hello. But no, this was North Korea (silly Wendy). He wanted money for my sins:

LOCAL HANDLER, *FRESH HANDLER* translating: The monk says the last time an American Imperialist visited this temple, he felt so ashamed of himself for the damage his American Imperialist bombs caused to the temple in the war, that he gave lots of money to feel better.

ME, *to myself, feeling an improbable mix of apoplexy and apathy:* Are you fucking kidding me? (*Then out loud.*) Please let the monk know that I'm an American, not an American Imperialist, and that wasn't my war. I wasn't even alive. I don't advocate violence of any kind. I don't even kill bugs! And in all my years of traveling to dozens of Buddhist temples around the world, never has a monk tried to extort money from me. Oh, and please let the monk know I said a prayer for him inside.

Put a fork in me. I was done.

ALICE STARTED TO HER FEET, FOR IT FLASHED ACROSS HER MIND THAT SHE HAD NEVER BEFORE SEEN A RABBIT WITH EITHER A WAISTCOAT POCKET OR A WATCH TO TAKE OUT OF IT, AND, BURNING WITH CURIOSITY, SHE RAN ACROSS THE FIELD AFTER IT...

LEWIS CARROLL

Alice's Adventures in Wonderland

PROLOGUE

It's amazing how badly you want to go outside when you're not allowed to. It was such a nice night in Pyongyang, and all I wanted to do was not be stuck inside my dim, drab, smoky, weird, empty hotel.

My handlers and I had just arrived back at the Koryo Hotel. It was only 6:00 p.m., but since foreigners aren't allowed to leave their hotels without their handlers, I wouldn't be allowed back outside until 7:30 a.m. the next morning, when they returned to fetch me. I felt like a dog with a shock collar on.

I moaned, "I feel like I'm being sent back to prison."

Older Handler recovered quickly and volunteered to take me on a walk.

"Meet in the lobby at 6:55; walk from 6:55 to 7:05."

Itineraries and meeting times are very strict in North Korea.

We walked two long blocks up and two long blocks back, with people staring at me the entire time—clearly not happy to see an American Imperialist. We stopped in front of a tiny enclosed stand. Older Handler asked me if I'd like to try a North Korean ice cream "special treat." I declined, ruminating over the likelihood of an actual, real ice cream stand existing in the barren retail wasteland that is North Korea (*probability*: zero).

She was not having it. "You said you feel like you are in prison. Eat the ice cream!"

Her feelings, I guess, were hurt. I ate the ice cream, which tasted kind of like an orange Creamsicle, but without the cream, or the orange.

Depositing me back at the hotel at 7:05 p.m. on the dot, she turned and said to me, "There. Now you feel better," like I was some kind of child who had been granted a magical five-minute ice cream mind-eraser furlough.

Yup, all better.

I asked (again) why the main hotel for foreigners couldn't just put a bench right outside the front door—right by all the guards and doormen—that tourists could sit on for fresh air and not be stuck inside the hotel all the time.

She responded in typical North Korean fashion (*read*: insane), "To be honest, because naughty Americans—but not you—are using this information to create false stories about our country to make it look bad, so not until the reunification of our country."

Right, got it.

Coincidentally, we spent the next two days in the countryside at hotels that had benches outside in small courtyards inside the hotel grounds. Older Handler was very quick to emphatically point out the benches to me, repeatedly letting me know I should sit there so I "wouldn't have to feel like [I] was in prison." By this point in the trip, I couldn't tell whether she was trying to be helpful or just spiteful. I think it was a little of both.

I am and have always been a traveler. Exploring the world, meeting its people, experiencing their lives, and sharing what I see are my greatest passions. I've traveled to more than eighty-five countries—including territories and colonies—many of which I've been to multiple times, and I'm struck more and more not by our differences but by our similarities. Beneath all the trappings of politics and religion, and apart from variations in the way we live our daily lives, I have come to understand how fundamentally the same we all are as human beings.

Then I went on holiday to North Korea. And like Alice in Wonderland, I fell through the rabbit hole.

This is my tale.

HOW DO YOU KNOW I'M MAD? SAID ALICE. *YOU MUST BE*, SAID THE CAT, *OR YOU WOULDN'T HAVE COME HERE.*

LEWIS CARROLL

Alice's Adventures in Wonderland

CHAPTER 1

ARRIVAL

I t was June 25, 2014. Air China Flight 121 touched down at Pyongyang's Sunan International Airport and taxied to a stop on the tarmac. The cabin door opened. I disembarked the airplane and descended the passenger boarding stairs. I was alone, a tourist in the Democratic People's Republic of Korea, unaccompanied by an organized tour group or international liaison (unlike most other visitors to the country).

I had never been more excited.

Aside from our plane, twelve or so fellow passengers, the half-dozen soldiers and airline employees who'd met us at the bottom of the stairs, and a giant smiling portrait of Kim Il-sung affixed to the side of the terminal building, the area was completely empty. There were no baggage trains, no food or fuel trucks, no conveyor-belt vehicles, or vehicles of any kind for that matter. There were no ground crews doing their jobs. There were no other planes. We were it.

One of the soldiers pointed me in the direction of the terminal building. I walked to the entrance and went inside. That twenty-foot walk to the terminal's entrance would mark the last time I was allowed outside alone for the next ten days.

The inside of the terminal was as devoid of normal airport activity as the outside was—something I would have expected had we just landed on a small island in the Philippines or a dirt runway in Uganda but not in the capital of North Korea.

There were three booths for immigration: two for "regular" people and a third for diplomats and other government officials. As if it was inconceivable that a foreign woman would travel alone to North Korea and *not* be a diplomat, my fellow passengers kept urging me to join the diplomatic line. I stayed put. I didn't want to risk deportation trying to impersonate a diplomat when I hadn't even been *im*ported yet.

When it was my turn, I walked up to the counter, laid my papers and passport down, smiled, and chirped, "Hello!"

The agent grunted back without making eye contact.

He took one paper from me, stamped another, and handed it back with my passport, and I was in.

I was euphoric. The most exciting moments in my life, when I feel most alive, happen when I'm touching down anywhere in the world I've never been. I am reborn into a new world, where everything is a curiosity to wonder at, and even the smallest accomplishment is a victory. There was nothing but discovery and learning ahead of me. And I was in North Korea—the most reclusive country on Earth. This was going to be amazing.

Even though I'd done research to make sure the size and type of camera and lens I'd brought would be acceptable, cleared my iPhone of any applications I thought might be questionable, and had declared all of my other electronic devices and cash on my immigration forms, I still felt trepidation as I approached security.

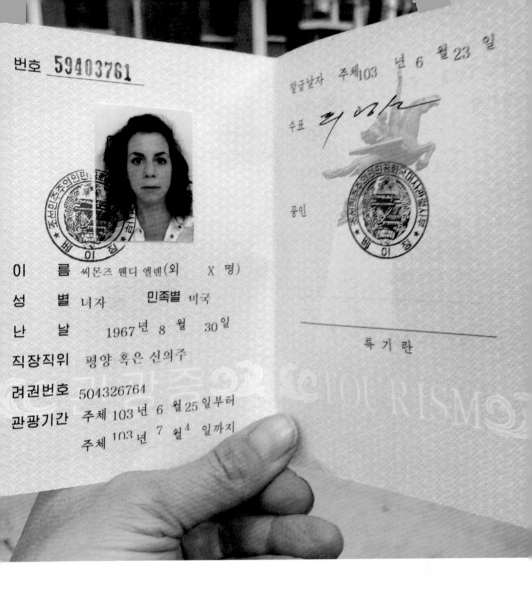

번호 59403761

이　　름 씨몬즈 웬디 엘렌(외　　X　명)

성　　별 녀자　　　민족별 미국

난　　날 　　1967 년 8 월 30 일

직장직위 　평양 혹은 신의주

려권번호 504326764

관광기간 주체 103 년 6 월 25 일부터
　　　　　주체 103 년 7 월 4 일까지

발급날자 주체103 년 6 월 23 일

수표

공인

특 기 란

"Cell phone!" demanded a guard.

I'd read online that North Korean officials take your cell phone and examine it but give it back nowadays, so I handed it over without argument. I put my bags on the baggage scanner, which looked about a hundred years old, and walked through the also-ancient metal detector. After being patted down, I stood watching as a gaggle of guards (soldiers?) huddled in a semicircle around my phone. I couldn't imagine what they were doing with it, since it was locked. Installing a listening or recording device? They were probably just trying to unlock it.

After a few minutes, a guard returned my phone and pointed to a set of doors, indicating I was free to go. But my luggage was still inside the baggage-screening machine. I pointed to the machine and politely said, "Bags?" hoping my luggage was merely trapped in the scanner's inner sanctum, not confiscated. When the guard realized what I was saying, he began shouting at the other guards, who in turn began shouting at one another as another guard worked to dislodge my bags. To slake the mounting chaos, I smiled and jokingly said, "Don't worry! Happens all the time!" I was summarily ignored.

Reunited with my bags a few minutes later, I emerged from security and was greeted by my two smiling, seemingly blissful North Korean handlers—the people who would be my near constant companions until I returned to the airport ten days later.

Older Handler stepped forward and introduced herself first. She was prim, wearing decades-old clothes that looked part *Star Trek*, part 1960s air-hostess uniform, only not stylish and in ugly colors. If we were the cast of a TV show, Older Handler would be the neighbor lady who always tries so hard to look put together *just* so but can't quite pull it off.

Older Handler then introduced me to her subordinate, Fresh Handler. Older Hander told me she was "fresh" at her job—that is, she'd only been a guide a short time. Fresh Handler was young and diffident, and something about her shaggy-punk haircut and sweet demeanor told me I'd like her best.

As Fresh Handler said hello, Older Handler unabashedly looked me up and down, sizing up—as I would be called throughout my trip—the American Imperialist. Then, without taking a breath, in a tone slightly less than suspicious:

You first time come Korea? You been South Korea? You been Japan? You speak Korean?

ME: Yes. Yes. Yes. No.

North Koreans' antipathy for Americans cannot be overstated. They are taught aggressively from birth that the United States is their number-one enemy, that Americans are imperialist pigs hell-bent on occupying North Korea, and that we may attack North Korea at any time. The Party espouses this rhetoric to maintain its absolute power over the North Korean people. If there is an enemy from which the people need protecting, the Party can be their protector.

We exited the airport, and I was introduced to Driver, who had spiky hair and was standing next to our car smoking. He half grinned, revealing several gold teeth, then took my bag and loaded it into the boot.

Older Handler directed me to sit in the backseat next to Fresh Handler and took the senior position in the front.

My "North Korea Is Great! America Is Not!" indoctrination began immediately. The car doors had barely closed when Older Handler uttered "our Dear Great Leader" and "American Imperialist" for the first time.

As we drove from the airport to our first tourist attraction, the Arch of Triumph, Older Handler turned to me with a smile plastered across her face and said, "Do you know what today is?"

ME: Umm, Wednesday?

(Which was true.)

OLDER HANDLER: It's June Twenty-Fifth, the day the American Imperialists invaded our country.

(Which was not true.)

On June 25, 1950, nearly the opposite happened. North Korea invaded South Korea.

Unsure what etiquette dictated in such a situation, I awkwardly said nothing, hoping the conversation would end. She asked me the question again, perhaps thinking I hadn't heard her the first time. I offered the same answer.

Unsatisfied with my response, Older Handler responded, her smile unperturbed, "It's the day your country invaded our country."

ME: Oh, that's a coincidence then that I arrived today.

I quickly glanced at Fresh Handler with a look that said, "Ack. How did I screw this up already?" And like the new best friend I knew she would be, she giggle-smiled back at me the equivalent of "Don't worry!"

33

I looked back at Older Handler, whose smile was now gone. Like a one-two-knockout punch, Older Handler said something to Fresh Handler and Driver, then Driver pulled the car over, and Older Handler and Fresh Handler switched seats.

Older Handler looked at me and said, "Now I watch you more."

Welcome to North Korea.

RULE FORTY-TWO. ALL PERSONS MORE THAN
A MILE HIGH TO LEAVE THE COURT.

LEWIS CARROLL

Alice's Adventures in Wonderland

CHAPTER TWO

CURIOUSER AND CURIOUSER

L ike Alice, I've fallen through a rabbit hole into a world full of strange and nonsensical events, where normal is surreal, lying is widespread, and the ruler has a penchant for demanding, "Off with her head!"

It's a world where what you don't know *can* hurt you, and ignorance is *not* bliss, where you must forgo all established logic to acclimate, and "Jabberwocky" makes sense.

But it's North Korea, not Wonderland, where I went to explore, with no Cheshire Cat to lay out the score. So I wrote this brief guide for readers and tourists, so my journey into madness won't seem quite as curious:

1. You are an American Imperialist, and North Koreans will call you this right to your face. They will also tell you that they "hate your country, and your leader…but not you," and that your country is responsible for all of their problems. Don't take it personally; they believe *every* word of it.

2. Everyone in North Korea calls North Korea "Korea" or "the DPRK," and North Koreans "Koreans." This is because North Koreans believe North Korea and South Korea are still one country and one people, and reunification would be imminent were it not for the

American Imperialists' occupation of the South. Calling North Korea "North Korea" or North Koreans anything other than "Koreans" just reminds everyone you're an American Imperialist, responsible for ruining all chances for the reunification of their country.

3. Visitors quickly learn that three Kims, not one, govern NoKo: Kim Il-sung (dead); his son, Kim Jong-Il (also dead); and his grandson, Kim Jong-un (the new fat one). You'll also learn you should never say *leader* without the qualifiers *dear, great* and/or *supreme* preceding it. Koreans seem to believe that these three terms are actually part of the word *leader*—like a hyphenated word—so if you just say *leader*, no one knows whom you are talking about.

4. Don't ask how old the new fat leader is or what year he was born, as it's considered impolite:

    M E : What year was your current Dear Great Leader born?

    O L D E R   H A N D L E R : To be honest, this question is considered impolite. (*Followed by tight-lipped smile that I quickly learned meant the conversation was over.*)

5. For that matter, don't ask or talk about the new fat one at all. No one seems to acknowledge his presence or give a shit about him, and there are only so many hours in a day (even if it feels like 2,000), so focus on the two great dead ones.

6. Koreans love both of their Dear dead Great Leaders…*a lot*. They love their dead Great Leaders as much as I loved my cutest, most adorable, best doggies in the whole wide world (coincidentally also dead, and running North Korea). Vibrantly painted murals (*read*: flat, desaturated, Technicolor-looking pastels) of the Dear Leaders commanding troops, running movie studios, and beauty-pageant waving while standing on the edge of active volcanoes punctuate NoKo's otherwise overwhelmingly drab, gray, washed-out world. Larger-than-life statues of one or both Great Leaders riding horses, dressed as farmers, or simply being big tower over cities and towns and are there to greet you everywhere you go. It is the cult of Kim, and fierce, absolute, unalloyed love and loyalty are demanded (and shown), or stiff penalties must be paid. Whether you encounter larger-than-life Kim(s) in the library or in a forest, before doing anything else you must first reverently and respectfully bow before the statue (hands to your sides, sunglasses off, no photos or talking

until bowing complete) until your guide cues you that the time for idol worship is over.

7.   As mentioned, Koreans believe their first Dear dead Great Leader is still running the country—literally calling the shots—from his glass-encased mausoleum inside the Kumsusan Memorial. In fact the North Korean people refer to Kim Il-sung as their Eternal Leader—and in addition to him being an all-around amazing human being and one awesome guy, Koreans will proudly tell you he is also their sun (as in *shine*) and their father (as in *dada*...ism). Do not laugh. It's one hundred percent true. They swear to Sung.

8. As if they're not busy enough running the country while dead, and being gods and the sun, etc., the Great Leaders are also expert geniuses at literally everything. Whenever mortal man is in a bind, a Dear Great Leader (living or dead) needs simply to show up, stand, and point—officially referred to as providing "on-the-spot guidance"—and presto chango, all is great. Just like that of their fictional superhero counterparts, the preternatural genius of the Great Leaders knows no bounds. They effortlessly dispense expert advice on everything from hydroelectricity and satellite technology to proper desk height and SPFs. Every place you visit during your trip—from the hospital to the dam (which the Koreans call the Barrage)—has the Dear Great Leader's on-the-spot guidance written all over it, usually in the form of a commemorative plaque (red writing on paper in a frame) or some kind of monument (red writing etched in concrete walls, red writing etched in rocks), which you will stand staring at while your handlers or local guide retell His Supreme Genius's genius advice, given at that very spot. Try not to think too hard about why such a supreme genius can't sort out the country's chronic lack of toilet paper, water, electricity, and food. This too is considered impolite to ask about.

9. Be it the statues, murals, monuments, or commemorative plaques, or the billboards, signs, posters, paintings, or photos that dot every spot—from street corners to schools, parks to stamps—propaganda is *everywhere*. Taught in school, enforced at home, played on the radio, blasted from loudspeakers day and night. Only government-approved books, art, film, music, and fun exist. No freedom of the press, no internet, no outside news, no outside *anything.* Unless it's Great Leader love (specifically, how great and smart the Great Leaders are, how great and smart the Great Leaders are at being great and smart, and how great and smart the Great Leaders are at giving genius on-the-spot guidance) or how strong and powerful their military is (particularly when crushing the American Imperialists), or how disgusting and despicable the U.S. and South Korea are (just in general), or how pleasing and fantastic

their lives are in North Korea—basically anything other than propaganda simply does not exist, and it will be force-fed to you from the moment you arrive until the second you leave.

10. Koreans have adopted a calendar system predicated on Kim Il-sung's birthday instead of Jesus Christ's. Year one is 1912, the year the Dear Great Leader was born, making 2014 year 103, 2015 year 104, and so on. They correlate his birthday and other important dates in his life to all kinds of things: the length of a road, the number of floors in a building, the number of lines in a poem, and how many people can fit in an elevator. Your local guides and handlers will often say things like, "The poem on this rock is written in three lines of forty-eight characters each because our father, who is our sun, was born on this day." They will also tell you in what years and how many times a Great Leader has visited every place you go. If you add the Great Leader's birthday to the number of places he's visited and multiply by the years, you can probably calculate pi.

11. If you want to push your handler's buttons, ask about the giant elephant in the room, the Ryugyong Hotel. This towering pyramid, which defines the Pyongyang skyline, has been under construction since the 1980s and still isn't finished. This is particularly curious because, according to your handlers, every other structure erected in North Korea, regardless of size or complexity, took no time at all to build.

DAY ONE

Cut to: immediately upon arrival anywhere in North Korea, when Wendy was still being polite.

OLDER HANDLER: To be honest, this building is 600,000 square meters and took three weeks to build.

ME: Wow. That's very impressive.

DAY SIX

Cut to: immediately upon arrival anywhere in North Korea. Wendy, no longer so polite.

OLDER HANDLER: This building is 800,000 square meters and took one month to build.

ME, *to myself*: Huh, that seems pretty unlikely. There's absolutely no way you were able to build this gigantic thirty-story building in only thirty days since you have no power tools or electricity or running water. On the other hand you are a country of slaves, so I guess it's possible your Dear Great Leader could have just said, "Hey, you 300,000 normal people are going to do nothing for the next thirty days but build this building, and I don't really care how many of you die doing it." (He probably whispered that last bit.)

So, it's equally likely that it's true, or not true, which is the fundamental conundrum with everything everyone says to you in North Korea, and it will slowly make you crazy.

ME, *aloud*: Uh huh. That's pretty fast.

OLDER HANDLER: Yes.

ME: So then let me ask you this…what's the deal with that pyramid hotel? I mean it's been under construction for what, like 30 years? Why can't they get it done? What's the holdup? I bet it's still completely empty inside! Have you been inside? But you're a guide…surely as a guide they'd want you to see inside. When will it be finished? Why wouldn't they tell the guides? I just don't understand. I mean if they can build an entire movie studio in a week, why can't they get one hotel finished?

OLDER HANDLER, *while making a sweeping, grandiose arm gesture*: Who can know the future?

ME: Well, I thought your Dear Great dead Leader could?

OLDER HANDLER, *VERY tight smile.*

12. Unless you're inside your hotel, where you're free to roam alone, you will never be without your handlers and usually your driver. And every place you go, you and your handlers and driver will be met by local guides, sometimes one, sometimes a few, sometimes many.

So at each of eight to ten activities scheduled for every single day (I was on a solo private tour, so this could be different for people on group or preplanned tours), you are suffocated in bombast by entirely new groups of people. As a single person who lives alone because I like it, I found this, above all else, to be one of the hardest parts of my trip. I could not wait to get back to my room at night so I could decompress from ALL THE TALKING *AT* ME.

13. You can take photos of almost anything you want in Pyongyang. This is because Pyongyang is the Workers' Party of Korea's gleaming showcase city. Even so, the Party and your handlers do their best to keep your movements restricted to the official tourist routes, and almost everything is staged, and the following photographic subjects are strictly forbidden:

   a. anyone in the military
   b. traffic ladies
   c. stores
   d. empty shelves in stores
   e. people waiting in lines of any kind
   f. errant litter
   g. normal people outside your regular propaganda tour (unless you ask permission)
   h. anything that isn't staged (i.e., anything unscripted or unplanned that accidentally happens during your propaganda tour)
   i. anything your handler thinks *you* think will make a great photo
   j. me eating dinner in the banquet hall of the Koryo Hotel.

Conversely, you are not allowed to take photos of anything outside of Pyongyang without prior authorization from your handlers or local guides because the rest of the country is a primitive, third-world shithole. You will entertain yourself devising ways to thwart this.

14. Everyone in North Korea lies to you about everything, all the time. Doesn't matter what, who, or why, or whether it's small stuff or big stuff. And when they aren't outright lying to you, they're either purposely unclear, or evasive—or if they really object to what you're asking or saying, they'll just pretend you aren't talking or they can't hear you.

   Cut to: Older Handler, Fresh Handler, and Wendy standing in the driveway of the Koryo Hotel, waiting for Driver to pull the car up. It's raining.

   ME: Sad. It's raining.

   OLDER HANDLER: Very lucky. Nice sunny day.

   ME: It's raining.

   OLDER HANDLER: No.

   ME: Yes, it's raining. See?

   OLDER HANDLER, *tight smile.*

15. Everything in NoKo is the same everywhere. Everyone wears the same 1950s-era clothing or uniforms. All the local guides have the same hairstyles and speak in the same urgent whisper. All the buildings have the same basic decor. It's all the same marble, the same wall coverings, the same chairs, the same tablecloths, the same bicycles, the same uniforms, the same smiling portraits of the dead Great Leaders, the same bowls and the same beer.

16. Bring only small-denomination bills as spending money—euros, RMB, or U.S. dollars will do—because there is no change in North Korea. By small, I mean *small*. By no change, I mean *no change*. Even so, more than once I was given bottled water as change for small-denomination bills.

17. Whether you're on an independent tour, as I was, or a scheduled group tour like most everyone else, everything you do in North Korea is nearly flawlessly scheduled in advance by the Korean International Travel Company (KITC). The company meticulously plans for and prepares every detail of your hour-by-hour itinerary with military precision, making sure everything is in place and everyone is on script, so you will leave North Korea believing it's the best place on Earth. They are the ultimate event planners. Whether it's a tour of the Fatherland Liberation War Museum or a visit to an orphanage, the KITC has it covered. But, as you actually are on Earth, interruptions will occur, and when they do, DISCUSSIONS will be had. The length and severity of said DISCUSSIONS are wholly dependent on the nature of the anomaly. Arrive someplace and the local guide is sitting down instead of standing up: a threatening grunt or two will do, as the guide jumps to his or her feet like the chair has suddenly caught fire. Wendy deciding at breakfast she doesn't want to go to the town of Sinchon to visit the Sinchon Museum of American War Atrocities: CODE RED! DIS-CUSS-IONS! And since there are no cars on the roads, or lines to contend with anywhere, the KITC can control time, too, choosing to schedule start times on less commonly used increments like 7:55 a.m., 1:35 p.m., or 6:55 p.m.

18. There is no need to account for lines or crowds, because no place is crowded, because no one is there. Okay, sometimes people are

there, but it's never one or two people or a small group of friends just casually hanging out talking or taking in the sights. It's a flash mob, NoKo style. Say you arrive at a Funfair (one of NoKo's extraordinarily depressing amusement parks), and there's no one there. Within minutes of arriving, a huge swarm of people—usually hundreds—will suddenly arrive, always walking in lockstep, five or six people across and as many deep. And of course they're dressed and look nearly the same, sporting the same decades-old clothing and hairstyles, many, sometimes most, wearing military or other uniforms. Your handlers may deny this is happening, even when you point to it while it's happening. In such cases, deny their denial and continue asking *a lot* of questions.

PEOPLE IN NORTH KOREA WALK
IN LINES LIKE THIS:

AND LIKE THIS:

19. Your handlers will take excellent and overbearing care of you. It's their job. They are tasked with ensuring you have a perfect experience and that you leave loving the Great Leader and North Korea. Basically they are (not) paid to brainwash you. This makes your interactions with them complicated and difficult. As a fellow sentient being, you will experience profound feelings of sympathy and empathy, while simultaneously feeling annoyed and disgusted by their blatant attempts to ingratiate themselves. Your options are to not think too hard about their feelings, motivation, lives, future, and mental states and enjoy your time, or drive yourself insane and rack yourself with guilt. I went with the latter. I recommend the former.

20. And finally, every place in NoKo is dimly lit (if at all), so keep your cell phone handy.

IT'S REALLY DREADFUL, SHE MUTTERED TO HERSELF, *THE WAY ALL THE CREATURES ARGUE. IT'S ENOUGH TO DRIVE ONE CRAZY!*

LEWIS CARROLL

Alice's Adventures in Wonderland

CHAPTER THREE

THE KORYO HOTEL

I am sitting alone in an enormous banquet hall inside the Koryo Hotel, waiting for someone to serve me dinner. I'd been directed to sit at table number eighteen in the center-right of the room for no discernible reason. This is where I am first introduced to what I will learn is the prevailing style in North Korea: fancy tacky.

The room is beyond garish, with terrible fluorescent lighting (somehow made worse by strands of something slightly resembling Christmas lights but not in the right colors, and a whole lot less festive) and tables dressed with clashing 1970s-hued, tuna-pink tablecloths, lemon-yellow placemats, and lime-green napkins—all of which are dirty. Overly dramatic, bellicose-sounding, anthem-like communist music blasts from speakers plucked straight from the 1950s. In the ensuing days I spend in North Korea, I will come to understand that (1) almost everything in North Korea seems plucked straight from the 1950s and (2) I will almost never not hear that music blasting from speakers.

My waiter arrives, and somehow we discover that we both speak Spanish. From then on, *hablamos en español sólo*. There are no words to describe how horrible his accent is, except perhaps *horrible*—it was damn bad. And through no fault of his own, he keeps bringing me small plates brimming with food that is both indescribable and inedible. I'm a vegetarian, so I know that it takes a special talent to fuck up eight plates of vegetables. No longer hungry, I ask if I am allowed to take my "Large

Beer" up to my room to drink. (You are automatically served one free Large Beer with lunch and dinner. However, you must ask, and pay, for water.) "Sí," he replies with a smile that is both kind and genuine. My Spanish-speaking waiter will turn out to be my best North Korean friend, after Fresh Handler.

Life at the Koryo Hotel was like watching a Wes Anderson movie only weirder, and I was the star. Like the dining room, the rest of the hotel is decked out in decades-old decor that in its heyday was gaudy, chintzy, and ostentatious, and in the present day is dated, faded, and démodé. A little less dirt and a little more quirk and you might call the place kitschy, but the pervasive feeling of melancholy and doom that envelops the hotel made that ship sail.

I spent five nights in the Koryo, two of which were consecutive, all of which were in my assigned room: 2-10-28. When I left my room on, say, Tuesday morning, and there were four squares of toilet paper left, and one of the lightbulbs in the bathroom had burned out, and the soap had melted to a sliver, and half of my Large Beer sat atop the ungainly nightstand-cum-AM/FM-radio-cum-alarm-clock next to the bed, two nights later, when I returned, all would be exactly the same. Only another lightbulb in the bathroom would have burned out. By the end of my stay, there were no lights in the bathroom. All of the bulbs had burned out.

I asked Older Handler why it was that I was put in the same exact room each time we stayed in the Koryo (my handlers stayed in the hotel, too, even though they lived in Pyongyang) and why they didn't freshen my room in between stays. Older Handler replied, "You can leave your suitcase for $25," typifying the inane, illogical, insane, absurd, and/or evasive responses I'd receive to all questions, except when people would just plain lie to me instead.

That North Korea has widespread electricity shortages is well known and well documented, but there is still something truly eerie—and oddly hilarious—about stepping off an elevator onto a floor in pitch darkness. It's too late by the time you realize. The elevator doors close behind you, and there's no going back. It's just so damn dark. Your eyes don't adjust, and you can't find the button to summon the elevator. It's abject blackness.

Unprepared the first time, I stood there in the dark, laughing at what a caricature of itself NoKo is, as I searched my bag for my flashlight—a.k.a. my cell phone, which was useless otherwise, save for the *Kaplan Vocab for GRE* app that required no internet or Wi-Fi to work. (I learned 169 new words during my trip.) And because it feels like I'm bullying NoKo if I point out that there was no consistent way to unlock my door using the electronic key, which often left me standing in the pitch-black hallway, cradling my phone under my neck as I tried inserting the key in every possible direction until somehow the door magically opened…well, I won't do that then.

The gift shop in the Koryo Hotel lobby—which is really more of a bodega that also sells ugly clothes—provided my primary sources of sustenance: milk-chocolate bars and bottled water. It also, inexplicably, sells large pieces of frozen fish, which I often thought about bringing up to the register as a joke. But since I was already doing America no favors with my behavior, I refrained.

One day when we were driving around Pyongyang, I noticed a modern building that looked inhabited on an island in the middle of a river. (Rule of thumb I came to realize: dilapidated, old building = real building with actual DPRK inhabitants; modern, new building = fakery built to make NoKo look normal.)

"What's that?" I asked innocently.

"Hotel," Older Handler snapped.

I pressed on, a lamb to the slaughter, "How does that hotel compare to mine?"

"Yours is fine," she barked back through her conversation-ending, tight-lipped smile.

I realized at some point during my second day that everyone was always wearing a pin with one or more of the Great Leaders on it. At first I thought it was just the handlers, drivers, and other people interacting with tourists, but no, it's all DPRK citizens except for children, who are not considered citizens until age seventeen. (When I asked Older Handler what you're considered from birth until age seventeen if not a citizen, she responded, "a child." Fair enough.)

Fascinated by a law that requires citizens to wear pins depicting their dead leaders (albeit dead leaders the people believe are still ruling the country posthumously) at all times, I peppered Older Handler with questions about what would happen to you should you be unwilling or unable to wear your pin. The last round of our lengthy and rather useless exchange went like this:

> **ME:** Okay, but, what if your house caught fire, and when you ran outside to save yourself, you forgot to put your pin on first?

> **OLDER HANDLER,** *being deliberately obtuse*: I don't know such a day.

Victory, hers.

One afternoon the elevator guard stopped me from entering the designated tourist elevator. Since he was the same elevator guard who was always there, and I'd stayed in the hotel three nights already, and been up and down the elevator a million times, and was clearly a tourist—not to mention there were maybe twenty-five tourists total staying in the hotel that week—I'm pretty sure this guy knew I was a legit guest and was just fucking with me. Nevertheless, I showed him my key as proof.

He refused to budge. He just stood there, arms crossed. I was in no mood. Without a second thought, I gave him a look that said, "Are you fucking kidding me?" while accidentally saying aloud, "Are you fucking kidding me?" Whoops. So I added, "C'mon dude, I have to pee." Without saying a word, he stepped aside and waved me past.

Victory, mine.

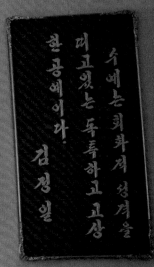

NO, NO! THE ADVENTURES FIRST, SAID THE GRYPHON IN AN IMPATIENT TONE: *EXPLANATIONS TAKE SUCH A DREADFUL TIME.*

LEWIS CARROLL

Alice's Adventures in Wonderland

CHAPTER FOUR

JAMES FRANCO COULD HAVE KILLED ME

'm standing at the sink brushing my teeth in my hotel bathroom, which looks like a motel bathroom from any movie made in the 1970s that involved drugs and bell bottoms, but with worse lighting.

It's my first morning in NoKo, and I've been instructed to meet my handlers downstairs in the lobby at precisely 7:50 a.m. I set my alarm for 7:00 a.m., but I hadn't needed it. Turns out some kind of eerie patriotic-murmur-music starts playing out of loudspeakers every morning around 7:00 a.m. here in NoKo—I guess to cheer workers off to work. When I asked Older Handler about it, she told me she didn't know what I was talking about.

The Koryo has cable TV with international news channels, a true luxury anywhere you travel, let alone in North Korea. Because the TV is in the other room, the sound is a little faint—but I'm pretty certain I hear the BBC broadcaster say that North Korea is threatening war against the U.S. over the forthcoming release of a Sony Pictures movie called *The Interview*, about two CIA spies plotting to kill Kim Jong-un, starring James Franco and Seth Rogen.

Umm, whaat?!

I dash into the other room to catch the story. Oh, THIS IS TOO GOOD! It's hilarious! The Supreme Leader of North Korea has promised "merciless retaliation" against America over a James Franco movie fewer than 24 hours after I arrived!

I plop down on the bed and wait for the news cycle to loop through so I can watch the story again. When it comes back on, it includes actual clips from the movie that has pissed North Korea off so much that they've decided to declare war. I'm pretty sure this is ironic. It's definitely funny, at least, with my being an American in North Korea and all. Because my mom watches the morning news, there's little doubt in my mind she's just shit herself.

Perplexed by why the Hermit Kingdom is allowing an American Imperialist to watch something on the hotel TV that is so egregiously offensive they'd declare war against America, I think to myself, huh, maybe these guys aren't so bad after all. That thought doesn't last long, though, since a second later the screen goes black, and I realize that a TV censor somewhere has probably "lost his job."

UPDATE

I first heard the news about the James Franco/Seth Rogen movie and North Korea's retaliation threat on the morning of June 26, 2014 while in North Korea. On the morning of November 24, 2014, a picture of a grinning skeleton with a warning message that said, in part, "We've already warned you" appeared on Sony employees' computer screens. This would mark the onslaught of an unprecedented computer hack on Sony by a group calling themselves the Guardians of Peace (GOP). Within days of the hack, which cut Sony off at the knees, rumors began to circulate that the attack was in response to the forthcoming release of *The Interview.*

Although there was no firm evidence yet, on June 26 NoKo warned that the film's release represented an "act of war" that would lead to "merciless retaliation against the U.S.," which I remembered hearing verbatim in my hotel room in Pyongyang. Crazy!

In the ensuing weeks the GOP leaked to the public vast amounts of crippling and embarrassing information stolen from Sony and issued a statement confirming that the hack was a result of the movie.

Following threats on theaters, several cinema chains decided not show the film, Sony announced it would cancel the Christmas Day release, and U.S. intelligence officials conclusively linked the GOP attacks to North Korea, which of course denied any involvement (but praised the Sony hack as a "righteous deed").

Then all hell broke loose.

President Obama went on record saying "Sony made a mistake" by deciding to pull the film, and Americans were outraged that a two-bit dictator could successfully impose censorship on American society... over a comedy no less.

At first North Korea volunteered to help find the "real culprit" behind the hack but then decided the United States government was behind the making of the movie and threatened to attack the White House, the Pentagon, and the entire U.S. instead, which prompted President Obama to declare that the U.S. would "respond proportionally."

Eventually Sony did an about-face (peer pressure? publicity stunt? dollar signs?) and released the film on Christmas Day to any theaters that wanted to screen it and to homes via video on demand. Obama praised Sony's decision (the people were heard!), and the movie raked in over $15 million in online downloads in just four days, making it the number one online movie ever released.

Take that, NoKo.

Ironically, while millions of Americans were downloading *The Interview*, tens of North Koreans (okay, a thousand at most) lost access to the internet when NoKo's service went down. In retaliation, Kim Jong-un called President Obama a monkey.

Many have questioned how a country with no electricity could pull off such a grand hack. To those people I say, because it's a batshit-crazy country full of slaves.

The story broke on June 26, 2014, my first morning in NoKo. I started writing this book on November 6, 2014. I finished the first draft the morning of December 18, when the story couldn't be any hotter, then boarded a flight for Sri Lanka. I missed the movie's release because I was in Ella, Sri Lanka, where the power had gone out (as a result of excessive rain and landslides, not an evil dictatorship), so I couldn't access the internet. And on January 3, at the end of my trip, when I arrived at the airport to fly home, the U.S. announced sanctions against NoKo in retaliation for the hack.

미국의 핵전쟁도발책동을 짓부시자!

I SEE NOBODY ON THE ROAD, SAID ALICE.

I ONLY WISH I HAD SUCH EYES, THE KING REMARKED IN A FRETFUL TONE. *TO BE ABLE TO SEE NOBODY! AND AT THAT DISTANCE, TOO! WHY, IT'S AS MUCH AS I CAN DO TO SEE REAL PEOPLE, BY THIS LIGHT!*

LEWIS CARROLL

Through the Looking-Glass

CHAPTER FIVE

SHIT I THINK MIGHT BE REAL

fakarant (*noun*). Any location that resembles a restaurant in that it has tables and chairs and place settings and waitresses, and prepares and serves food, but is not a restaurant in the anywhere-else-in-the-world sense of the word because:

I.   It seems only tourists eat there

2.   All of these places seem to be operated by the KITC, a company whose express goal is convincing tourists that NoKo is normal. In this case, their job is to persuade visitors that there is a plethora of restaurants in Pyongyang and that normal Koreans can, and do, eat in them whenever they want to (which they can't and don't).

Only once did I see anyone other than tourists and their handlers in any of the fakarants. One night in Pyongyang we went to a fakarant for dinner that had several small, private dining rooms instead of one main room. As we were being shown to our room, we passed a group of Chinese tourists. Older Handler pointed and said, "They're Korean." (They were not. Or they were, but they were missing their telltale Great Leader pins, were speaking Chinese, and their KITC van was parked downstairs next to our car, which I saw with my own two eyes when we walked out.)

Anyway, we are on our way to a fakarant for lunch, and Older Handler turns to me and says that since I like to take photos, would I like to go to a real Korean wedding?

Are you kidding? Of course I would!

This is so nice of Older Handler, I think to myself. I'd like to believe she's just being nice—even now I can barely type this next bit without my heart falling—but there's *no way* she's just being nice. Of course she's ingratiating herself to manipulate me in some way. And it's been a particularly boring, fascinating, disgusting, and hilarious morning of North Korea, WINNERS, America, SUCKS! So she may also be trying to throw me a bone.

But I don't care about the reason. If she's giving me the chance to see something even approximating her version of real, I'll take it.

It turns out that the son or daughter of an employee of KITC (the story, as usual, was convoluted) was conveniently having his or her wedding reception that very day at 1:00 p.m. at the same fakarant where we were having lunch at noon. On a Thursday.

I was skeptical.

We arrived at the restaurant, which interestingly had a "shop" on the ground floor. Shops, like restaurants in North Korea, are confusing, and hard to come by. I hadn't seen one yet, and we'd spent a lot of time driving around Pyongyang. I'd been peppering Older Handler with questions about shops—where are they, could she point one out to me, when are they open, who could go, what are the hours, do people walk up and down aisles, do people push carts, do people choose things from shelves or do they take whatever they're given...the same type of questions one might ask Martians or a three-year-old, to which Older Handler simply replied, "Yes." So when she saw one, she took the opportunity to point it out:

> **OLDER HANDLER,** *while pointing to the dark, closed, near-empty shop that from what I could see primarily sold large stuffed animals and very cheap fancy clothes*: See, there's a shop.

We walked up the stairs, past the fakarant's filthy, disgusting guest bathroom. Think worse than a dive-bar bathroom at the end of a long night, including unidentifiably wet floors, while remembering there is no running water in most bathrooms. I wasn't concerned about myself; I've been going to the bathroom in literal shitholes (and worse) all over the world (including the U.S. of A.) my whole life. But all I could think about was, "We're at a wedding! That poor bride! With her long dress! Or maybe she has a short dress? No, probably not. How will she go to the bathroom in that bathroom and not get her dress wet? Will she not go to the bathroom during the reception? How can she not have to go to the bathroom? Maybe it's a short reception? What kind of reception is on a Thursday afternoon anyway?"

We're immediately directed to our table (no crowds, no wait), and as we dine, several waitresses busily go about setting up the room for the reception. It's fascinating; they manage to move fast and slow at the same time. They're beautiful—(I read somewhere later, after getting home, that the Party selects the most fetching women from around the country to come live and work in Pyongyang so the city literally looks its best for foreigners), and they're setting up one of the ugliest rooms I've ever seen. To start with, it was painted the color of Grey Poupon mustard.

There were also the wrong holiday lights of course, this time shaped like a Christmas tree I think, and pink balloons to match the pink-and-blue napkins, and gold-beige-covered chairs. There were pink-and-purple, cone-shaped, tulle-draped flower stands with giant bows around their skinny necks and snowman-size rose bouquets for heads. There was a large flat-screen TV—for entertainment, I suppose—and twenty or so cases of beer stacked along the wall next to the bridal table. The table was covered by an elaborate floral arrangement with a heart at its center, in which sat stuffed teddy bears (man and wife—guessing newlyweds) dressed like pilgrims. There was also a real, dead stuffed bird on the table next to the pilgrims. Which species of dead bird, I cannot guess.

But the thing that really caught my eye was the individually wrapped towelette packets included at every place setting. Aside from the fact they were even using individually wrapped towelette packets as part of the place settings at a wedding (although the etiquette rules on this may be more lax for weekday daytime weddings), they seem to have been taken from Air China, or so the labeling led me to believe. Perhaps tourists who failed to use theirs on their flights casually gave them to their handlers, who amassed them over time, and they found themselves at a wedding.

We'd long ago finished lunch and had been sitting there for a while. The reception was delayed. My handlers were bored to pieces, yet I'm still riveted by the simple machinations of table setting and party preparation going on.

By now my handlers are slacking off a bit—a combination of being tired from a very busy morning, boredom at sitting waiting, and a shared Large Beer at lunch. Their lack of attention emboldens me to take more photos of more things without worrying about getting caught.

The photo I sneak of a waitress standing casually in the kitchen, with her left leg bent just a touch, waiting for something at the counter, is the photo that breaks the camel's back. First I get into trouble...no more photos (now I'm bored), then the waitress does (unfair rebuke...I'm the one with the camera, after all).

Several people enter the restaurant and DISCUSSIONS take place. It prompts me to wonder if and how many DISCUSSIONS must have taken place for me to be sitting there bored in the first place.

Older Handler keeps me updated: bride and groom delayed, bride and groom arriving. Then she tells me to stay standing at the back of the room.

The guests begin arriving, both men and women (Older Handler explains that some wedding receptions are male- or female-only), and they are all dressed in their regular NoKo attire. That is, whatever they would have been wearing five minutes ago if they were *not* going to a wedding was what they were all wearing now. Men dressed in military uniforms? Check! Men dressed in short-sleeve work shirts and pants? Check! Ladies in their *Mad Men* costumes? Check! Children in school uniforms? Check! The only thing missing was semiformal, formal, or cocktail attire. Unfortunately Older Handler has also informed me that I'm not allowed to take any photos of the guests.

So I'm hanging back, trying to look casual and be as unobtrusive as an

American Imperialist can be while crashing a wedding in North Korea. Older Handler tells me to get ready, that the bride and groom are on their way! I feel like a paparazzo waiting for the money shot. But I'm a little confused about how I'm supposed to take a photo from the back of the room.

When the bride and groom cross the threshold, the logistics are made clear: Older Handler drag-pushes me straight through the middle of the crowded room, (conveniently) making it impossible for me to take photos of any guests, before depositing me directly in front of the bride and groom, who are standing behind the bridal table.

I may be struggling to find true north in this land of uncertainty, ambiguity, and doubt, but the bride's unmistakable glare upon seeing me—a clearly unwelcome and uninvited American Imperialist with a camera in her hands—proudly earned the first spot on my "Shit I Think Might Be Real" list. Followed second by the wedding reception…I think.

I am allowed perhaps five seconds to snap this photo of the happy couple before being ushered out of the fakarant faster than a president is pushed out of harm's way during an assassination attempt.

ALICE LAUGHED. *THERE'S NO USE TRYING*, SHE
SAID: *ONE CAN'T BELIEVE IMPOSSIBLE THINGS.*
I DARESAY YOU HAVEN'T HAD MUCH PRACTICE,
SAID THE QUEEN.

LEWIS CARROLL

Through the Looking-Glass

CHAPTER SIX

AND THEN THERE WERE TWO

We pull up to the front gate of the Paeksong Food Factory in Pyongsong for my scheduled tour. When no one meets our car, Driver begins to honk with ever-increasing urgency and yells furiously until the military chick meant to be guarding the entrance stumbles out of her booth, disheveled and abashed.

It quickly becomes clear she is both out of uniform *and* has been sleeping. I am beyond entertained as I watch her hurriedly try to pull herself together (hat on, shirt buttoned up and tucked in, halter/belt thing on, etc.) while she frantically runs back and forth from the gate to the factory. I'm no expert on the NoKo system of rule, but I'm pretty certain that being out of uniform is bad, and being asleep even worse, but *both*? Ouch. Her cartoonlike scrambling is amazing and immediately makes my "Shit I Think Might Be Real" list.

After three or four sprints to the inside of the factory and back, she enters and exits her booth one last time, then lifts the gate and motions us inside. As we step out of our car to an empty parking lot, we are met by the local guides and the factory manager. It's then that Older Handler tells me the shocking news: A mere *five minutes* earlier, the factory un-expectedly lost power, forcing it to close and send all 5,000 employees home. We will still be allowed inside, but there will be no people to see and nothing working.

A group of Brits who happen to be visiting the factory at the same time seem to enjoy peppering their handlers with questions they must know will result in inane answers:

> **BRIT:** So, all 5,000 people have just left the building five minutes ago and gone home then, or are they all waiting in the lunchroom for the power to come back on?

> **LOCAL GUIDE:** Yes.

Having spent some time in factories (and not being a complete idiot), I, too, can smell a ruse. All the surfaces, machines, and equipment are pristine. It seems unlikely—nay, impossible—to manufacture the purported plethora of products on the same two lines with just a few different machines. And all 5,000 people left mere minutes ago, and there isn't a single shred of physical evidence that even *one* human has ever worked here? Except for, of course, the napping guard.

But more importantly, I'm pretty sure if the factory she is single-handedly tasked with guarding *did* just lose power one- to four-and-a-half minutes ago, causing it to unexpectedly close down and send 5,000 workers home (or be held in the lunchroom), she would be fully clothed, or at least awake, if not both.

Lest you think I doubt the veracity of Older Handler's claim based on the actions of one unkempt, napping guard and solid housekeeping, on our approach to the factory on the only road in, we hadn't seen a single person coming the other way. Certainly there had to be a straggler or two. Someone with a limp?

My bewilderment grows once our tour of the factory begins. I am so stupefied by the factory's "control room" that I forget to take a photo of it. First, there are no electronic displays or control panels of any kind anywhere in the room. Second, *there are no electronic displays or control panels of any kind anywhere in the room.* There are: two barren desks; four chairs; and three dormant "monitors" affixed to the wall that I would swear aren't real but rather are those fake molded plastic-prop flat-screen monitors used by home stagers, realtors, and furniture stores. That's it. There aren't even pencils in the room. I don't believe anyone's ever *been in* this room, let alone controlled factory operations from it only minutes ago.

Next comes the Showcase of Products Room, which begged the question I kept finding myself asking of NoKo: If you're going to go to all the effort to put your "best foot forward," why not try a little harder to make it look better? Which is not to say the white-lacquer bookshelf-cabinet all-in-ones lined up next to each other along the wall and the bevy of beverages in clashing packaging didn't look pleasing; it just could've looked better.

Unexpectedly we come upon two workers who have, for some reason, stayed behind to finish making the biscuits after their 4,998 coworkers so quickly departed. The local guide or factory manager (I can't remember who) declares these workers "heroes."

We watch them—their heads down, doing nothing—for a few minutes, and then my group moves on. As usual, I stay behind watching, wondering what it all means. And as usual, Fresh Handler, always patient during my extended reveries—stays with me. Eventually one of the workers looks up and stares right back at me, and then she gives me the stink eye—my second stink eye in as many days. But it's also one of the few genuine things I've encountered. So I snap her photo, adding it to my "Shit I Think Might Be Real" list. And to Fresh Handler's great pleasure, we move along.

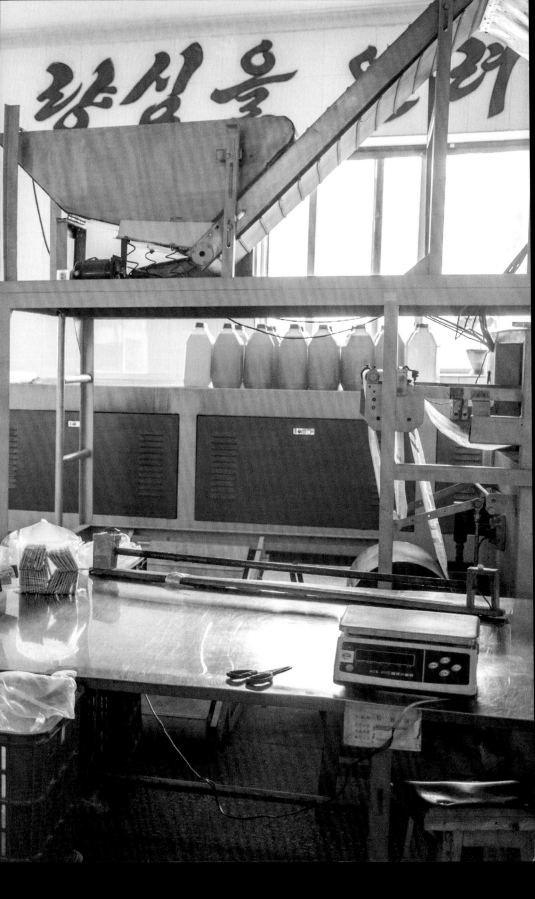

COME, WE SHALL HAVE SOME FUN NOW!
THOUGHT ALICE.

LEWIS CARROLL

Alice's Adventures in Wonderland

CHAPTER SEVEN

THE SIMULATION CINEMA

There was a change to our schedule, so we had an hour to kill before lunch and our afternoon drive to Kaesong.

"Waterpark?" Older Handler suggested.

"I don't have a bathing suit," I said. Never in a million years had it crossed my mind to bring one with me to North Korea.

"You rent one," Older Handler shrugged.

Ewwww. "No!" I shot back, perhaps too quickly. But the thought of sharing a rental bathing suit in a country that lacked running water held little appeal.

I abruptly changed tack, attempting to maintain our precarious détente, "That sounds fun, but I don't know how to swim," I lied.

"3-D movie?"

That sounded easy. All I'd have to do was sit and keep my clothes on.

"Great!" I replied enthusiastically.

A short ride later we pulled into the empty parking lot of the Runga Funfair, "A Wonderland for the People!" next to the Taedong River.

It was closed, I guess for the day, but it looked more like it had been abandoned forever. I could practically see the tumbleweeds rolling by. As I stood taking photos of nothing, my handlers entered into intense negotiations—DISCUSSIONS—with the employees sitting inside the glass booth at the entrance. Eventually Older Handler tells me to pay a euro, and we're allowed in.

As we walk through the deserted amusement park toward the Simulation Cinema, Older Handler keeps insisting the Funfair is normally open seven days a week and is always very busy.

I don't know what to say.

"Then why is it closed now?" I ask.

> OLDER HANDLER: They didn't know we were coming.

> ME: What did you just say?

> OLDER HANDLER: The people, they come later.

> ME: What time does it open?

> OLDER HANDLER: Yes.

Good chat.

When we arrive at the theater we are, as is often inexplicably and arbitrarily the case in NoKo, required to cover our shoes with oversize, opaque, blue, protective caplike things like the ones doctors in operating rooms are required to wear on their heads to cover their hair. The trouble is, in NoKo these things are themselves dirty, having never been washed, and you put them on over your shoes while still standing outside, then walk from the outside in, thereby eliminating all chance of keeping the outside out.

And there I am—standing in the lobby of an empty movie theater in an abandoned amusement park in North Korea, surrounded by handlers, wearing blue protective personal equipment over my feet to prevent contamination.

We walk over to the ticket counter, which looks more like a desk, and I'm instructed to pay. It costs four euros, but I only have a five-euro bill. What happens next is a bona fide shit show. No one is prepared to make change! No one told them I was coming! Making change is not on the schedule! You can't just get change for a five-euro bill any old place! This is North Korea!

An urgent and unpleasant-sounding exchange takes place as I stand there impotently, confused by who exactly is in trouble for not having the correct change: me, my handlers, or the cashier.

Abruptly, Older Handler turns to me and barks, "You get change after movie." That answers that. I'm the one in trouble.

We walk through the lobby and into the tiny theater.

There's a small rack off to the side where I'm told to put my day bag. Since all of my money plus my camera and cell phone are in my bag, there's no way I'm leaving it unattended off to the side in a darkened room. "That's okay. I'll hold it," I say.

"But the movie is very dangerous," Older Handler replies.

"What the *fuck* are you talking about?" I think but I'm pretty sure don't say out loud.

Sensing my uncertainty, she clarifies, "The movie…it moves."

Ah, I get it. It's one of those 3-D immersion movies where the seats move in tandem with the film.

"That's okay. I'll hold it on my lap."

Undeterred, she stands staring with her trademark tight smile, waiting for me to capitulate.

In that moment I have the profound realization that Older Handler is actually as annoyed with me as I am with her. Still, there's no way I'm leaving my bag.

There are two elevated rows, five seats across, and I'm astonished to see people sitting in each. If my handlers are likewise surprised, they aren't showing it, but Older Handler moves quickly to reorganize the seating chart, and three comfortably seated moviegoers are jettisoned from the theater.

Sorry about that.

As we take their seats and fasten our seatbelts (!), the man sitting next to me asks where I'm from. I smile and tell him America. Then he asks if it's my first time visiting Korea. "It is," I answer cheerfully. "Do you like Korea?" he continues. "I do (not)!" I respond, incredulous that we're allowed to speak freely. I wonder how many rules he's breaking, and I start fearing for his safety.

Older Handler stands up and walks out, ostensibly to fetch our 3-D glasses, but moments later she returns with a man who says a few words, and then the entire audience of North Koreans stands up and leaves.

"Why did everyone leave?" I ask, already knowing the answer.

"Wrong movie," she replies.

Thirty-five minutes of logistics behind us, we put on our plastic yellow 3-D glasses, and the movie, a race-car-themed film called *Winner*, begins. Our seats vigorously shake and pitch forward and backward, as we narrowly avoid crashes and fly off cliffs.

Fresh Handler squeaks and squeals, "Ooohh!" She's legitimately enjoying herself ("Shit I Think Might Be Real" list). And I've got to admit that Older Handler was right; hanging onto my bag with all of the jostling and lurching is not at all easy.

The movie lasts maybe four minutes.

The lights come up, and I smile at Fresh Handler, who's so cute and sweet wearing the clunky, ill-fitting, yellow-plastic 3-D glasses. "Did you like the movie?" I ask. "Oh, yes!" she answers enthusiastically. I love her.

I turn to Older Handler and ask her the same thing. "I feel sick," she says and stands up to leave.

We walk back through the lobby and out the front door, where we pause in front of the theater to remove the anti-outdoor-indoor-contamination shower caps from our shoes.

We make it a few more feet when a voice beckons us to stop. It's the cashier from inside with my one euro in change.

WELL, NOW THAT WE HAVE SEEN EACH OTHER,
SAID THE UNICORN, IF YOU'LL BELIEVE IN
ME, I'LL BELIEVE IN YOU.

LEWIS CARROLL

Through the Looking-Glass

CHAPTER EIGHT

NEXT STOP: NORMAL PEOPLE

was sitting on the Pyongyang Metro interrogating Older Handler. As usual, I was trying to get to the bottom of things.

> **ME:** Who are these people on the subway?

> **OLDER HANDLER:** To be honest, normal people.

This was how it would go. She would reply to my question with such absurd nonsense that I would either have to just suck it up and stop asking questions or prepare to dig in, and let the baby-talk roll. But getting past her rehearsed lies—no matter how reductive my questioning—was impossible. And this exchange was no different.

And from what I've been told, "normal people" must work Monday through Saturday (Sunday is their day of rest, but they must do volunteer work then for the Party). It's midafternoon on a Thursday, and this place is packed. And since there are no dry cleaners, or shops, or banks, or other errand-type places, and the only let's-do-lunch crowd in town is me, I'm hard pressed to understand exactly who all these "normal" people are.

> **ME:** Why aren't they at work?

OLDER HANDLER: They are.

ME: Then why can I see them?

OLDER HANDLER: Yes.

Unfortunately, Q&As in North Korea are a zero-sum game.

Some people probably find digging for answers fun. But I find the painfully slow extraction of information from an unwilling and therefore purposely obtuse source to be aggravating as all fuck—especially when that someone, in this case Older Handler, had an unbelievably ironic vocal tic of starting half of her responses with, "To be honest…"

I am on an "Extended Ride on the Pyongyang Metro," which meant I was allowed to visit four (no longer surprisingly) dimly lit stations—this, despite the large number of elaborate chandeliers and light fixtures housed in each. And like everywhere else in North Korea, each station had that familiar mix of rousing, communist-era music and urgent-sounding talk radio blasting out of loudspeakers. Each was adorned with heavy-handed propaganda (murals, mosaics, carvings, and statues) extolling the virtues of NoKo's values and Great Leader love.

As we stood on one station's platform, an old wooden train rattled into the station, and people who I guess were commuters opened the manual doors.

ME: So that guy over there who just opened the door…is he just like a normal guy, going to or from work?

OLDER HANDLER: Yes, work.

We step into the car, which is nearly dark, illuminated by a single fluorescent bulb at the other end (and of course by the smiling portraits of the two Great dead Leaders), and stand right in front of the doors. A group of what must be at least a billion Young Pioneers (schoolchildren who are members of the Children's Party, easily identified by their red kerchiefs), who I guess are taking a field trip, come running for our car but stop comically short at the door when they spot me. They stare at me, giggling, too afraid to board. Is it because I'm a MILF?

Oh right, I'm an American Imperialist.

One brave Pioneer finally breaks rank and boards our car, to the ceaseless laughs and jeers of his friends. The pressure too great, he alights seconds later, he and his troop choosing to forgo the ride rather than stand next to me. I feel like a pariah. He makes my "Shit I Think Might Be Real" list.

When the train stops at another station, I encounter yet another billion Young Pioneers, and a King-Kong-size, illuminated statue of a Dear dead Great Leader (a King Kim?) beckoning all of his children to exit the platform to his left.

The Pyongyang Metro has twenty-one (known) stations, configured in two bisecting lines that form a simple X.

  ME: Why can't we see any of the other stations?

  OLDER HANDLER: I show you map.

  ME: Yes, but why did you choose these four stations to show me?

OLDER HANDLER: To be honest, these are the stations our Great Leader has visit.

ME: Do all the other stations look the same as these? Do they have the same type of fancy lights and decorations?

OLDER HANDLER: Only under construction.

At yet another station, men and women were gathered around stands protruding from the floor that looked like flagpoles, but with newspapers instead of flags. Older Handler explained that they were reading the news (Party-issued propaganda intended to convince the people that their Great Dear Supreme Leader is great).

The train that ferried us to our last station was crowded. We actually had to push ourselves on and into the car, like normal people do on any normal subway, in any normal city, on any normal workday.

ME: I just don't understand who all these people are. Like why would those three teenagers be on here alone instead of in sch---.... You know what, forget it. (I decided to sit this one out.)

Standing there, squeezed between real people—one of the rare times I encountered them during my entire trip—I make eye contact with an old woman. She grins and makes that universal half-nod, half-stand, wave gesture that means, "Please take my seat." I decline, smiling, and nod silently to say, "No, no, you sit, please."

But we'd both made our move at the same time (I'll go left. No, *I'll* go left.), and the millisecond of confusion was a crowd pleaser. The people surrounding us burst out in laughter! I mean three people giggled, and a couple of people covered their mouths and smiled. BAM! Pull out the "Shit I Think Might Be Real" list again.

And even though the metro is the first place in all of NoKo where I encounter what I consider to be free-roaming people (they're weirdly dressed, yes, but they're not walking in a veritable spreadsheet of persons, four people across by eight people down, like I've seen elsewhere/everywhere on my trip), and they appear to be taking normal rides, I can't shake the feeling that something's off.

The Party tries to control one hundred percent of what you see and do in NoKo, so most of what you see is at least *mostly* staged, and anything completely real *wasn't supposed to happen*. So things that seem normal or should be normal, just aren't. And normal-looking things are fucked up in the weirdest way, or weird in a really fucked-up way.

There's what the powers that be want you to see in North Korea, and what they want you to think (or believe—and are these the same things?), and it's all gray territory from there. So unless you're taking it all at face value or dismissing everything out of hand, you spend an inordinate amount of time mentally navigating the gray areas.

And I was finding it exhausting. So exhausting, I thought to myself, I should have taken that old woman's seat.

*I THINK I SHOULD UNDERSTAND THAT BETTER,
ALICE SAID VERY POLITELY, IF I HAD IT
WRITTEN DOWN: BUT I CAN'T QUITE FOLLOW
IT AS YOU SAY IT.*

LEWIS CARROLL

Alice's Adventures in Wonderland

CHAPTER NINE

IT TAKES A HERO

Weird-looking yet oddly beautiful trees caught my attention while we drove the length of the Youth Hero Highway from Pyongyang to Nampo. Both my handlers had dozed off, and I had my headphones plugged into my phone, which meant I could sneak a few photos through the window without making a sound.

The Youth Hero Highway, Older Handler had eagerly explained before dozing off, is so called because it was built by "youths"—that is, DPRK citizens under the age of 30—who had "heroically" built the highway in service to their Party and Great Leader. Sounded pretty good so far. Then she added, almost as an afterthought, "and many, many youths went blind." *Now* the story had taken that familiar NoKo turn.

Wait, what?

"Did you say *blind*?"

She smiled tightly, "Of course." (*Read*: Clearly, Wendy is an idiot.)

Alarmed but undeterred, I pressed ahead with what I thought was a fairly logical rejoinder, "Why did so many youths go blind building the highway?"

"Because of the dynamite (you fucking moron)," she replied with her trademark tight smile.

Riiiight…my bad.

Actually by now this was my bad. Why *wouldn't* the youths go blind from the dynamite while building the highway? It's not like I'd seen any power tools or eighteen-wheelers or men wearing safety goggles, or whatever else we've come to expect in construction zones. Hell, even the men I saw building roads in the middle of Congo wore hard hats, and they lived in huts made of cow dung and straw.

She continued, "To be honest, our Dear Great Leader was so proud of the youths who sacrificed so much for the good of our country, he visited the highway and decided to make the men heroes and name the highway in their honor."

But that's not all!

"When our Leader make the youths heroes, all the women want to take care of them or marry them."

Win! Win!

She beamed and said, "The Youth Hero Highway is Korea's crowning achievement!"

From where I sat, I would say the Youth Hero Highway was definitely better than an unpaved road.

According to Older Handler, "The Youth Hero Highway was built from 2000 to 2002 and is 260 *ri* long." It was intentionally built that length because "2/60 is the birth of our Great Leader," she explained, adding that 260 *ri* "is being equal to 88 kilometers."

According to Wikipedia the Youth Hero Highway was built from 1998 to 2000 and is just 46.3 kilometers long.

No sense quibbling over facts, given the reliability of both sources.

Here is what I observed: the Youth Hero Highway is ten to twelve lanes wide and is an unmarked, uneven, pothole-ridden asphalt blacktop (reminiscent of elementary-school playgrounds circa 1974–1979) that has, of course, no vehicles.

Well, there were *a few* other vehicles, but from what I could see, they were either filled with other tourists or with people in uniform who I assume were military or important enough to be on the road. Otherwise the highway was empty on both "sides" and on our drives both to and from Nampo.

When I asked why there were no cars on the highway, Older Handler smiled tightly and said nothing.

Maybeeeee…abject lack of freedom of movement, and checkpoints at either end of the highway (and one in between) to enforce said lack of freedom of movement (at each checkpoint, guards scrutinized credentials that my handlers and driver were asked to provide, which Older Handler told me proved they were allowed to travel). And—for the win—no one is allowed to own cars.

And that's not even the weirdest part.

All along the 46.3 kilometers (I'm going with Wiki) were thousands (tens of thousands? hundreds of thousands?) of men on both sides of the highway, dressed in either military uniforms or clothing styles from the 1940s and '50s, cutting down trees *by hand*. By that I mean they were using things like small saws and axes, and saws where one guy holds one end and another guy holds the other end, and picks that look like the mallets doctors use to test your reflexes…cutting down trees. No electric saws or large machines—because they don't have any.

So there are thousands and thousands of men using their might to cut down 46.3 kilometers' (times two) worth of trees that are just flopping into the middle of the highway. Because it doesn't matter, because there are no cars. And it's a football field wide.

And as many men as there were cutting down trees, there were two to three times as many napping on the fallen trees and surrounding grass. Maybe the Dear Great Leader had come for one of his famous on-the-spot-guidance visits and declared that more naps on the job would make it suck less. Or maybe they knew that no matter how hard they worked or how much they accomplished, their low position in North Korea's rigid and unforgiving Songbun caste system had banished them to tree-cutter status for life…so, why not take a little nap?

Many to most of the trees looked recently planted. Confused, I asked Older Handler if the trees were being planted or cut down.

"Cut down," she said, smiling.

"Why are they cutting down so many thousands of trees?" I asked, having seen the exact same thing—trees being cut down by the shit ton—on a different highway the day before.

Her response: a tight smile.

A LARGE ROSE-TREE STOOD NEAR THE ENTRANCE OF THE GARDEN: THE ROSES GROWING ON IT WERE WHITE, BUT THERE WERE THREE GARDENERS AT IT, BUSILY PAINTING THEM RED.

LEWIS CARROLL

Alice's Adventures in Wonderland

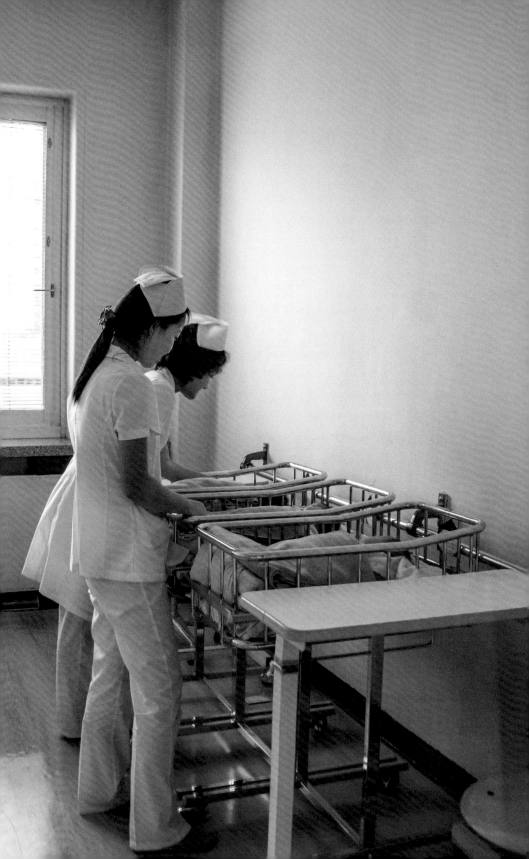

CHAPTER TEN

HOT DOCTOR, DIMLY LIT

After donning our ill-fitting, heavily soiled lab coats and our never-before-washed shoe covers—which for once are actually appropriate, given that we're standing inside the Pyongyang Women's Maternity Hospital instead of, say, the 3-D Simulation Cinema—we are allowed inside the front door.

As we stand in the not-bustling, or lit, or warm (even in summer) lobby, dressed like children who are dressed up like doctors, waiting for our local guide who will conduct our tour, Older Handler boasts that more than six million women have given birth in the hospital, including more than 8,000 foreigners. "Many foreigners have praised our Great Leaders for their care, because here treatment is free for our people with special medicine, and many foreigners are famous people." I'll have to take her word for it, since I'm having trouble believing that "many" famous foreigners, let alone one, would choose to give birth here.

When our local guide arrives, I fall in love immediately. It's a girl crush. She's literally the prettiest person I've seen in Korea, and possibly ever. She's maybe in her early twenties, with a model-worthy face and a perfect pout. She's wearing a fairly standard, bright-white, fitted nursing uniform, including a very old-school nurse's cap. When she introduces herself as Dr. So-and-So, an ob-gyn, I'm a bit surprised, if not duly impressed. She's hot, and smart. So what if she's wearing the wrong uniform?

Our tour commences: my ragtag team of handlers and I, partially dressed as poorly kempt doctors, plus the gorgeous Dr. So-and-So disguised as a nurse.

Our first stop is the lobby where we've been standing, to admire a ball-room-size, gold-colored chandelier above us, and the elaborate red-and-green-marble, flower-patterned floor below. "One hundred and sixty-five tons of rare stones were used to create the pattern," one of the handlers tells me. I guess the Great Leader, who I'm told has on-the-spot guidance-d all aspects of the hospital, thought these medically necessary accoutrements were well worth the spend. They definitely explain why all of the lights in the lobby are off. Budgets can be a bitch.

We stop next to admire a life-size painting of the smiling Dear Leader and his Great Leader son, both standing on the edge of what looks like Crater Lake. When I ask why their Dear Great Leader is pointing while standing Crater Lake-side instead of pointing while standing near, say, a gleaming iron-lung machine, they ignore me, and we move along.

I'm hard pressed to accurately describe what comes next. We enter a room lined with tiny booths like the kind you see on TV or in movies when the visitor talks to a prisoner who is sitting behind glass, only minus the glass. The trapezoid-shaped booths' stark, dank, floor-to-ceiling Arylide-yellow bleakness cannot be overstated.

I am directed to booth number seven, where I'm invited to sit at a desk in a clown-nose-red chair. Above me dangles a single bare bulb, which was probably turned off, but I can't recall.

I'm told to pick up the rotary-telephone-style handset hanging next to me on the wall. "This is for father communicating with new mom and see baby," Dr. So-and-So explains, as an ancient CCTV surveillance camera on the far wall clicks on and a black-and-white, midcentury-looking television encased in the wall below it gradually sputters to life.

"I don't understand," I say confused, "Can't the dad just go upstairs to see his wife and new baby? Surely the baby's father and family and friends can visit Mom and her new baby up in her room?" Dr. So-and-So lets me know that would be a no, no, no, and a no, due to "unhygiene" reasons.

"How long before the father is allowed in the same room as his wife and new baby?" I ask, trying to make sense of the news. Dr. So-and-So's exact response escapes me now, but I remember thinking it was more time than a typical American vacation but less than the twelve to fifteen weeks before puppies are fully vaccinated and finally allowed to go to the dog park to play.

I pick up the handset when I see a nurse on the TV screen. She's purportedly sitting someplace upstairs but looks instead like she's on the far end of a short, wide tunnel. Nurse picks up a colorless handset on her end, but instead of speaking into (and over) the pervasive low static I hear, she simply waves. I wave back, and she hangs up her phone. Then the screen goes dead.

Dr. So-and-So next leads us through a door into a truncated hallway, on the right side of which are a few rooms behind windowed walls. In one room we observe teeny-tiny premature babies in glass incubators, watched over by a woman dressed like Nurse Ratched. In the room next door, I see a neat row of ten babies clothed in matching onesies and tightly bundled in matching blankets, lying face up on matching striped mattresses, all of which have been placed inside what looks like the large wire bagel baskets you see hanging on the walls of bagel shops in New York. The baby bagel baskets are on wheeled stands but seem to somehow also hang from a matching metal bar attached to the wall. Neither room is illuminated by anything but the sun.

A third room has three matching babies in baskets half-hanging from one wall—triplets, Dr. So-and-So tells me, before directing my attention to two sets of twins in incubators parked along the other wall. I watch two nurses inside the room coo and smile at the matching babies for a few minutes, before Dr. So-and-So redirects my attention to a low wooden table in the hallway outside the door. Two small, gold-colored cases sit atop a cloth doily neatly placed in the center of the table: in one, a gold ring for girls; in the other, a miniature gold dagger for boys. Both are "congratulations on being born a twin or triplet" gifts given by the Party to the lucky children.

It turns out twins and triplets are a big deal in North Korea, and families of both are therefore accorded certain privileges, which as best I can understand are thus:

- Mothers carrying twins or triplets or who have just given birth are flown to the Pyongyang Women's Hospital by helicopter from anywhere in the countryside
- One free gold ring or dagger per child is given at birth
- One free glass of milk per child per day until age 17
- One free glass of oil per child per day until age 17
- Something about how because triplets are considered lucky they are taken into the state's care and will live someplace else, without being a burden to their own families. I had no idea what Dr. So-and-So was talking about. But later in the week when we visited an orphanage in Nampo that was chock full of twins and triplets, her words would become disturbingly clear.

When I arrived back home in New York City I read online in several places that triplets are remanded to orphanages at the Great Leader's behest. An unfortunate convergence of superstition, paranoia, and the Confucian reverence for triplets—believed destined for great power—has the Kims convinced that today's baby triumvirate may be tomorrow's defenestration.

My tour with twins and triplets now finished, we move on to the really weird stuff in the hospital.

Inside the "Dentist Room" were three empty dental chairs, each surrounded by fairly modern-looking dental equipment, at least as far as I could tell. Dr. So-and-So explained that the Great Leader himself insisted the room be built because "pregnant women want get teeth cleaned." I guess women on the verge of giving birth, and those who have just done so, want nothing more than a cavity filled or a root canal performed. I asked how many women per day had their teeth cleaned in the room. "Many hundreds, but all come in the morning before you arrive," Dr. So-and-So responded.

Next I'm shown the "Tanning Bed Room," wide enough to hold two first-generation tanning beds and little else. Unlike the modern, cocoon-style beds where the "roof" is attached, the roofs of these beds hung down from the ceiling, high above their bottom halves. One bed was turned off or broken. The other, inexplicably turned on, cast an eerie purple-pink light across the otherwise dark room. Before I could ask, Dr. So-and-So quickly explained that their Dear Great Leader had the Tanning Bed Room installed because "pregnant women need Vitamin D when they must stay inside too long."

We stop to visit a treatment room that is empty save for two paper-thin single beds that look more like examination tables. Each bed is made up with blue-and-white-striped sheets that are positively cheery in the otherwise drab and depressing room full of antiquated, chill-inducing medical equipment not seen since the start of the Cold War. Straddling the top half of either "bed" is a removable, plastic-looking contraption shaped like a half-dome, covered with the same matching sheets…a nice touch. When I ask Dr. So-and-So what the fortlike thingy is, she curtly replies, "Treat legs" and moves me along.

My love for Dr. So-and-So is beginning to fade a little.

In one "laboratory," men and women who are dressed like pastry chefs sit dutifully staring at but not actually into microscopes that are still housed under their thick plastic covers.

It's theater of the absurd, NoKo-hospital style.

When we stroll through the "patient" ward, door after door opens into one matching room after another, each as overflowing with antediluvian medical equipment as it is devoid of people. "The patients, they all go home," Dr. So-and-So tells me, then adds—as if telling me one more time will somehow make it true—"Patients only come in morning."

We take an elevator and emerge into a brightly lit hall, which I'm told is the lobby of a new hospital that's been built adjacent to the old one next door. I feel like I've unwittingly entered and exited a time machine instead of an elevator. But that feeling doesn't last for long, as it seems the upgrade is purely cosmetic.

We go down a flight of stairs, and I'm shown into a closet-size room, at the center of which is what looks like a modern mammogram machine. Dr. So-and-So tells me the machine is very expensive, more than 30,000 euros, but their Dear Great Leader wanted them to have it "for the health of our country." Not too shabby of the big guy, I initially think, before it dawns on me: there's only one machine to screen every woman in the country, and it's not even plugged in.

I ask how one machine can possibly be sufficient? It's like she's not even trying to lie to me anymore when she blithely responds, "We do many exams." Perhaps my concern is misplaced. After all, I haven't seen a single female patient over the age of newly born, and I've been in the hospital for an hour.

While on the subject of preventing cancer, I asked Dr. So-and-So if doctors in North Korea collaborate or share research on breast cancer with doctors in other countries, since there's been so much progress made. She has no idea what I'm talking about. I try again. "Do your doctors confer with other doctors or attend conferences, or read case studies about new treatments or results from clinical trials?"

"No cancer," she says.

No cancer as in, "There's no cancer in North Korea," or perhaps, "No, cancer…" but then you decided to stop speaking? I'm feeling impatient but try to keep my mouth shut.

I can't.

I decide to dumb things down a bit. After all, she's an ob-gyn, not an oncologist, and I hate myself when I don't play nice. "How many babies do you deliver per week?"

"Babies? No." Dr. So-and-So blankly replies. I'm seriously going to fucking lose it. And now I have to go to the bathroom to boot.

"Yes. Babies. You know, the tiny little new people we just saw upstairs," I say while making a gesture to indicate *small,* then *up.* "Did you not introduce yourself as an obstetrician/gynecologist? Obstetricians deliver babies, do they not? Therefore, how many babies do you deliver per week?"

"No," the pretty one stubbornly repeats.

Okay…questioning over. I am choosing to remain my best self. And besides, it's not her fault; the elevator time-machine probably erased her mind.

We're back in the bright-white lobby—but I can't remember how, because now I'm preoccupied by my newly shifting reality that Doctor Pretty is likely not a hot doctor at all but rather a well-played stratagem, and I her dewy-eyed fool.

I ask for the bathroom, figuring that at least there will be toilet paper and running water for a change, since we're in a state-of-the-art hospital, after all. On the way to the bathroom, we pause in front of a staircase so Older Handler can quiz me as to whether I notice anything about it.

> **ME:** Umm, it's pretty?

That seemed a safe bet.

> **OLDER HANDLER:** The center is green!

She's right. It's a marble staircase overlaid with green jade.

> **OLDER HANDLER,** *proudly:* To be honest, green looks like waterfall flowing down because when our Dear Great Leader visited for on-the-spot guidance, he pointed and said, "The color green makes pregnant women feel all better! No more pain!"

So with that, the staircase in the brand-new hospital building was ripped out, and rebuilt with green jade. No expense spared.

ME: That's awesome. May I please go to the bathroom now?

Older Handler took me to the VIP bathroom inside a presentation room where I would be forced to sit through a 400,000-hour-long presentation detailing everything about the same hospital I'd just toured during the past hour.

The bathroom, by the way, had lights but no running water or toilet paper. Progress!

Before leaving I was asked to write my impressions of the hospital in a guest book. I was tempted to write "Hot doctor, dimly lit" but decided this was probably funnier in my own head.

Instead I wrote "It was lovely. Thank you," and signed a fake name, lest I do anything to personally contribute to Korea's version of *One Flew over the Cuckoo's Nest*. Then I turned and walked out of the hospital, my "sterile" lab coat and shoe covers still in place.

FOR SHE HAD READ SEVERAL NICE LITTLE
STORIES ABOUT CHILDREN WHO HAD GOT
BURNT, AND EATEN UP BY WILD BEASTS, AND
OTHER UNPLEASANT THINGS, ALL BECAUSE
THEY WOULD NOT REMEMBER THE SIMPLE
RULES THEIR FRIENDS HAD TAUGHT THEM...

LEWIS CARROLL

Alice's Adventures in Wonderland

CHAPTER ELEVEN

THE KIDS ARE ALRIGHT

I have been traumatized by a Children's Palace.

Once I figured out that it is not the awesome, free, "Great Leader rocks" after-school program for arts and sports that welcomes any child who feels like going ("Because our Dear Leader loves us and says the children are our future." No, Older Handler, Whitney Houston said that) but is instead a center for extracurricular excellence to be achieved through years of mandated and rigorous study—and is restricted to the country's most talented children and those of the Party elite—I no longer know which way is up.

I gravitate to children when I travel. It may sound overly simple, but children have always struck me as the soul of a country. There's usually no pretense with them. No matter what's going on in a nation politically or socially, or how focused on putting on a show for tourists everyone else is, children will show you the truth. They are who they are, and who they are is a reflection of their country.

I therefore make a point of visiting schools, orphanages, and small communities wherever I travel in the world in order to interact with children. Whether I'm able to play with them, observe their schools, or just take photos and share, it's an extraordinary way to break down boundaries and barriers, and helps foster communication and under-standing at a young age.

So I was excited when we pulled into the parking lot of the Pyongyang School Children's Palace, the first Children's Palace we were to visit (I had loaded up heavily on children-oriented activities when planning my itinerary). Our local guide, an adorable, well-mannered little girl who spoke no English at all, guided us up a few flights of stairs, through a long corridor, and down a short hall.

Things went North Korea immediately.

Want to know what it feels like to be ushered into a room of three rows of five young girls, seated, skirts on, legs spread, most wearing protective shoe covers with bows, and each holding a giant accordion? And who, as you enter the room, bust out a tune as if you've caught them by surprise?

Well, it feels fucking strange.

After having the same, "Oh, you just caught us in the middle of practicing this song (or routine) perfectly" experience five or six more times, I'm starting to suspect the obvious: that they knew I was coming, that my visit's been staged, that they've likely been practicing this routine for years. They're all just waiting for tourists like me (and Party leaders) to arrive so they can perfectly perform their routines, and if there are any mistakes made, DISCUSSIONS will ensue.

When we visit a calligraphy class filled with (I was told) three- and four-year-olds whose work would put the Great Masters to shame, the gravity of the situation becomes clear.

These palaces aren't large, splendid houses for leisurely learning; they're extracurricular-activity jails.

Children are assigned their activity or skill in the same way they will be assigned a job later in life. He'll be a singer, she'll play the accordion, and they will practice every single day of their lives.

Are the children of the Palace complicit in the grand ruse, or are they just having fun? They may be slaves to arts and culture, but at least they're saved from tilling fields. And how are their circumstances all that different from those of pageant children with their crazy moms, or budding young gymnasts who choose to forgo normal childhoods for Olympic dreams? Questions, as always…without answers, as usual.

I'm not enjoying the Children's Palace as much as I expected.

After an interminable variety show and musical performance by the Children's Palace's best and brightest, I'm ready to go. North Korea is the greatest country on Earth, score one. Children are the truth of a country, score zero.

We drive to Pyongsong and spend the night in a hotel where I'm asked upon arrival to tell them what time I would like running water in my room. I think carefully before deciding, because I'm only given a half-hour window. At my appointed time, there is no water. I'm too tired to care.

The next morning, after we tour Pyongsong's Central Square, some monuments, the Paeksong Revolutionary Site, and the Paeksong Food Factory, we drive to the Kim Jong-suk High School for an interaction I hope will resemble something closer to truth.

After we pull into the driveway and get out of the car, I spy a few young boys peeking out of various school windows at us—the brave ones, perhaps. When I wave hello and snap a photo, they all quickly jerk back inside before popping their heads out again. I am playing peekaboo, albeit with high school boys instead of toddlers. Apparently the behavior is universal. Even in North Korea.

The principal, a handsome and winsome man, was also acting as our local guide. He walked over to our car to greet us. There was something in the way he parted his hair, the blackness of his shoes, and the cut and shape of his uniform that made me keep thinking he would be better suited standing on the bow of a ship or the bridge of the *Starship Enterprise*.

He escorted us into the school, which was clean, and colorful in the North Korean chalky, muted way (imagine Pepto-Bismol pink as a paint color that was also available in blue, yellow, and green). But it was cheerful and encouraging, and thanks to the many windows, not terribly dark (there were no lights on anywhere), and Principal seemed genuinely proud as he showed us the school's math wall of fame.

Next we were led upstairs to observe an English class, supposedly a

normal class already in session.

I was ushered into the back of the classroom, along with quite a crew: Fresh Handler, Older Handler, and Driver; the same three British tourists from the factory, who happened to be teachers themselves; their Danish liaison/international guide, their two North Korean guides, and their driver; three to five other teachers (supervisors?); and the principal. The students were completely undisturbed by all the people and commotion. Guess they'd been part of this goat rodeo before.

The British tourists' Danish guide had pulled me aside as we were walking into the classroom so he could remind me what a rare opportunity this was for me to see "real people doing normal things." I tried to shake off the memory of yesterday's Children's Palace fiasco, so I could approach today's English class with an open mind. Then Danish Guide proceeded to tell me in specific, near minute-to-minute detail what we were about to see, making his advice a bit harder to heed.

The children (mostly boys with a few girls positioned at the head of the class) were attentive and mirthful as the teacher, outfitted in a

purple-polyester pantsuit, enthusiastically pointing-sticked her way through the lesson. I alternated between snapping photos and trying to read over the students' shoulders, as I naturally contemplated how much of what I was seeing was staged.

As Danish Guide had predicted, we were next invited to take turns coming to the front of the room to field questions from the class. I chose to hang back, as I'm strangely introverted in situations like these, and I wanted to observe and take more photos instead.

With the Great Supreme dead ones smiling brightly behind them, the Brits took turns fielding predetermined, rehearsed questions from the students, who took turns raising their hands for permission to stand. They asked about who the Brits were, and where they were from, and for help with the English lesson the teacher had planned.

Although the studio-audience members (the students) were obviously plants, and their questions clearly preplanned, the answers the Brits gave and the students' subsequent reactions could not be. I wondered how and why the powers that be would take such a risk?

Perhaps this anticipation of knowing that anything could happen because kids are kids, and even well-trained ones make mistakes and accidentally (or purposely) say the wrong (or right) thing at the wrong (or right) time, explained the nervous energy I sensed and the preponderance of handlers in the room. After all, out of the mouths of babes falls truth.

That familiar refrain was running circles in my head: What risks are they taking, anyway? If everyone in North Korea truly believes their lives are so great, and everything is so perfect, then what are they working so hard to hide? Everyone knows nowhere is perfect, so why not just let kids be kids, since most kids really are all right?

I snapped back to attention when the class burst into laughter. It seemed one of the Brits—who was, no joke, an English teacher—was having a tough time teaching the English lesson on the board. A closer look at the board showed why. Here's what was written:

That crazy tower in Pisa

Grammar (1) She said, "The school begins at 8:20 at
our school every day (change into reported speech)
(2) My mother wanted me to write a diary every day (choose make,
let, have)
(3) Rewrite using with "enough"
The food was too hot to eat

Maybe it made more sense in English?

It was during moments like these—surrounded by a plethora of minders, standing in a classroom wired with security cameras and populated with students who I believe had been media trained to within an inch of their lives—that I would wonder to myself, why couldn't they just get that last bit right? Surely they could have kidnapped or held prisoner someone with a better grasp of the English language who could have prepared a more intelligent lesson plan? Or when mankind failed, couldn't the Great Dear One just go there and point?

I decided to switch positions and move to the front of the room, just inside the open doorway, where I could see all the students' faces and reactions as they followed along.

They all seemed so happy and engaged. But wasn't this what they did every day? Perform for tourists? Did they have practice run-throughs and drills, like their Children's Palace counterparts? Was any real learning taking place here?

I wasn't going to let one highly polished, over-the-top performance by North Korean child prodigies ruin all NoKo children for me. These kids were belly laughing and guffawing and having so much fun, I refused to believe it was staged.

Another Brit who taught math took to the center of the room. I nearly shed a tear when he asked one of the students if he could calculate the square root of some number (which of course I could not), and the student immediately got the answer right. There was indeed hope for all of us yet.

I then noticed one student staring at me. He was sitting a few rows back on the left and was the only student wearing blue. When our eyes met, he held my gaze instead of looking down or away, and he smiled. I smiled back and gave a tiny, silent wave hello. Then I held up my camera and nodded to ask if he minded if I took his photo. He smiled back nodding that yes, it was okay, so I did, and then nodded again to say thank you.

It reminded me of a moment long ago when I was in Jaipur, India. I was sitting in the back of a car stopped at a light that was besieged by indigent children begging loudly for food and money. As they jostled one another to gain position in front of the rolled-up window where I was sitting, a tiny young girl managed to emerge in front. She stood there silently, staring at me, as the chaos continued around her. We held one another's eyes for a moment.

For whatever reason I held my palm to the glass, and then she held her palm up to mine and smiled. Time froze as we looked at one another, smiling, our hands held together, aligned through the glass. I burst into tears when I realized too late that the light had turned green and our car was speeding off, with no way to go back.

I remember that little girl vividly. I think about that moment to this day and wonder whether she remembers me, too. It reminded me then, as it always does now, that what I do when I travel matters.

I've had so many incredible life-altering moments when everything else just falls away—when all the back-and-forth in my head quiets down and all my questions and doubts recede, and I'm just there, sharing a moment. And for that moment, it's about as real as it gets.

When the tour ended, our troop of handlers and hangers-on filed back into the hallway. Fresh Handler and I made a quick stop in the bathroom, where for once there was running water—only this time it wouldn't stop, so the bathroom floor was a stinky, wet mess. I pretended I wasn't wearing flip-flops and took comfort in the fact that we would be heading back that afternoon to my second home, the Koryo Hotel, where I was lucky to have running water on demand.

Later in the week we would visit two additional Children's Palaces—a second, larger one in Pyongyang and one in Kaesong. Like the first one, these two were large, elaborate buildings; in the case of Kaesong, the largest and most beautiful building in town. And as with their predecessor, my visits to both were a sad yet weirdly entertaining reminder of what "all work and no fun" can do.

I remarked to Older Handler at one point how "funny" it was that the students we'd seen at the Kim Jong-suk High School seemed so authentically jubilant and exultant, whereas all the children in the Children's Palace seemed so dour and grim (unless they were "on" and performing; then there were giant smiles plastered on faces). Wouldn't one expect students in school to be sullen and bored, I asked, and children at play to be high spirited and irrepressible, not the other way around? "The children can learn what they choose" was all she would say.

Not content with her answer, I let my standard baby-talk, Martian-style interrogation roll, "So if I was a student, you're saying I could decide to play guitar if I wanted to?"

OLDER HANDLER: Yes, of course!

ME: And then, if after a few months I decide I no longer like the guitar and I want to switch and be a singer instead, then I can just switch? Just like that?

OLDER HANDLER: Yes! Of course!

I had my doubts.

ME: So if children are free to choose any activity they want, why

149

would anyone choose to play the accordion? The accordion has to be for, like, the kids who can't sing or dance, right?

FRESH HANDLER, *speaking playfully, but looking a little hurt*: Hey! I played the accordion!

Whoops. So much for diplomacy, thanks to my big mouth.

ME, *futilely trying to recover*: Really? The accordion is great!

I try to imagine adorable, pretty, smart, and I'm guessing popular Fresh Handler back in the day, stuck sitting on her chair, all smiles, legs spread, protective shoe covers with bows on, swaying back and forth as she pressed this key, then that key, of her giant squeeze box.

FRESH HANDLER: Oh, they are very popular here. All teachers must play them.

This sort of made sense, because Fresh Handler had at some point told me her mother or father was a schoolteacher.

I asked Older Handler what activity she'd participated in while growing up. She, too, had played the accordion. Nothing ever made sense.

Later in the week we visited an orphanage in Nampo. After putting on our filthy operating-theater safety-gear shoe covers, we walked through the hallways, peeking into rooms that were filled with children of different ages—from newborn to maybe three years old. It all seemed so natural and so right, in as much as any orphanage anywhere can be. There were nurses attentively watching over children as they slept or ate snacks or played freely.

But then I was led to the end of the hall and into the main playroom, where Older Handler pointed out groups of triplets and twins who I'm guessing couldn't have been more than three. I sat on the floor to say hello, but most of the kids were too reticent to even acknowledge me. Older Handler was eager to translate for the local guide how happy they were that their Great Dear Leader had come to visit and selected the children's uniforms all by himself. This was one on-the-spot guidance visit where pointing had seemed to make a difference, as the orphans' uniforms *were* super cute.

As I sat there trying to make eye contact and convince any of the children to engage, I wondered what their daily lives must be like for them to be so completely disinterested in me, an American Imperialist.

And as so often in the perfectly orchestrated musical North Korea had time and again proven itself to be, my question was answered, as if on cue, when the budding young thespians broke into a perfectly choreographed "spontaneous" song-and-dance routine, its grand finale a NoKo Bellamy Nazi salute.

*REELING AND WRITHING, OF COURSE, TO
BEGIN WITH, THE MOCK TURTLE REPLIED:
AND THEN THE DIFFERENT BRANCHES OF
ARITHMETIC—AMBITION, DISTRACTION, UGLI-
FICATION, AND DERISION.*

LEWIS CARROLL

Alice's Adventures in Wonderland

CHAPTER TWELVE

THE GRAND PEOPLE'S STUDY HOUSE

We are standing around a boom box circa early 1990s, listening to a bootleg Madonna cover of "American Pie" that she sang for the movie *The Next Best Thing*, in which she starred as a yoga teacher who has an out-of-wedlock baby with her gay best friend, played by Rupert Everett. That's some racy stuff for North Korea.

I'm in the audio/video room of the Grand People's Study House. The local guide, who is also our DJ, has, in consultation with the local guide in charge of this particular room, chosen the "Madonna CD" as proof that the Study House is in possession of all music from every country in the world.

While we listen to all four minutes and thirty-three seconds of the scratchy song play, I fruitlessly try to explain who Don McLean is and why one pirated song burned onto a blank CD that's placed inside a plastic jewel case with a crappy, worn-out copy of a random black-and-white Madonna photo (that's not even the right size) in place of actual authentic liner notes doesn't really constitute adequate proof that they own all music from every country in the world, or at least not as far as America goes. If true, couldn't they have chosen *Holiday*, or *Like a Virgin*, or one of her other hits? I mean the woman has had a lot of number ones.

There are thirty or forty more of the exact same boom boxes sitting atop as many matching desks, but we're the only ones using any. Just beyond the boom-box ghetto are more rows of matching desks, with a hodgepodge of old cathode-ray TVs atop. Clustered together are four Koreans with headphones on, each watching something different on their TVs. But once Madonna starts complaining about "taking her Chevy to the levee, but the levee was dry," all eyes are on me. Maybe they don't like this song either, or maybe it's just because the music is super loud, and they blame me.

The Grand People's Study House is North Korea's massive 600-room national library and center for adult learning that dominates the center of Pyongyang. It's also a monument to the first Dear Great dead Leader in honor of his seventieth birthday. The local guide (the one in charge of the overall building, not the audio/video room) has informed us that under the Dear Great One's expert on-the-spot guidance, the 100,000-square-meter edifice (which equates to approximately 1,076,391 square feet) took a year and nine months to build. For comparison's sake, the 104-story, three-million-square-foot, One World Trade Center (formerly known as the Freedom Tower)—presently the tallest skyscraper in the Western Hemisphere and fourth tallest in the world—took workers roughly fourteen years to build. And they had lots of power tools.

As has been the case so many times during my stay in North Korea, I'm feeling a difficult mix of emotions. On the one hand, this couldn't be any funnier. I'm in the audio/video room of the national library, one of the most important and learned buildings in town, listening to a fake, bargain-basement CD on a boom box as big as their TVs are ancient.

On the other hand I feel bewildered and sad because I'm standing in the audio/video room of their national library, listening to a fake, bargain-basement CD, on a boom box as big as one of their ancient TVs.

If this is what they're showcasing as excellence, *how bad must things be*?

In a reading room that is twice as big as the audio/video room are two or three students sitting at individual desks, which—the local guide in charge of the reading room tells the local guide in charge of the building, who tells Fresh Handler, who then translates for me—are new desks replacing the long, communal tables people used to have to sit at when studying or reading in the room. Local-local guide goes on to say that when their Dear Great Leader visited the room for an on-the-spot-guidance visit and saw his fellow Koreans uncomfortably bent over the tables, "he wisely and kindly decide height of tables need to be adjustable to make more comfortable to study because our father love us." So he invented adjustable desks.

If only he could harness his powers for good.

Purportedly, the Grand People's Study House can house up to thirty million books. I'm not sure whether it actually *has* thirty million books, because by the time the local-local guide in charge of the you're-not-allowed-to-see-the-library-library told the local guide in charge of the building, who told Fresh Handler, who told me, something may have been lost in translation.

The local-local guide is on the other side of the marble counter we're standing in front of, seated at a small, unadorned desk. Like most buildings we visit in NoKo, this one is built with a quarry's worth of marble. Next to her is a tiny book-size conveyor belt, sticking out a few feet from a tiny, square, book-size hole cut through the wall behind her.

Through our now well-established game of telephone, Fresh Handler invites me to name a book I'd like retrieved. "Any book?" I ask, astonished that this might actually be real! But it seems that Fresh Handler—being fresh and all—has misspoken ever so slightly, a teensy mistake she realizes she's made when I request *The Little Prince* (a classic, and one of the best-selling books ever that's been translated into a billion languages) and the buzzer says *no way*.

DIS-CUSSIONS!

"I mean *Huckleberry Finn*," she tells me I told her.

And whoosh! Out rolls a copy of *The Adventures of Huckleberry Finn* in a mini bin on the track. One look at the timeworn book, and I'm starting to think that the majority of the "millions" of books are out there in the ether with all the music.

We step into a smaller room, this one crowded with maybe eighty or ninety people (four of whom are women, the rest men), seated at rows of tables poring over computer screens. They seem to be learning some kind of CAD application, but I'm not sure because all of their screens look different, and no one is moving a muscle or talking—not even the person I'm guessing is the teacher, who's sort of half-slumped over at the head of the room (under, of course, large, smiling portraits of the Great Leaders), and particularly not the three men who have their heads on a table and appear to be sleeping.

I joke with Fresh Handler that I don't think the sleeping guys are going to be passing their exams any time soon, and that if those Great Leader portraits could see, there'd be trouble. She giggles. I ask Fresh Handler to ask the local building guide what the conscious students are studying, but she doesn't know. That's the local-local room guide's domain, but he/she is either missing or is the one not teaching up front. In any case, time was up for the computer room, so we moved along.

I don't recall the order of things, but I do remember that all of the hallways were poorly lit, and we did not visit a single room that had more than a quarter of its available lights on. In the gift shop, it was lights out altogether.

I also remember them telling me that more than 10,000 people use the Grand People's Study House every day. But as I walked the dark corridors, stood in the dimly lit lobby, peeked into dark rooms that were off the itinerary (Older Handler or the local guide in charge of the building were quick to shoo me away), and visited the dimly lit rooms that were on the itinerary, I saw no one come, no one go, and no one waiting for anything...not for books, not for elevators, not even to use one of the nine reference (?) computers randomly placed in the lobby near the front door (no chairs), which patrons are allowed to use to make you think North Korea has the internet. (I kid. I don't know what they use the computers for.) And I don't think I'd be going out on a limb to say the tote bag I purchased was the gift shop's sole sale for the day.

I had beers with an Irish doctor the last night of my stay, and we compared notes on our respective visits to the Grand People's Study House. We'd both visited the same rooms and seen the exact same things, only he'd been treated to Irish folk music and an esoteric Irish medical textbook of some sort instead of Madonna and *Huckleberry Finn*, proving without a doubt that there are at least two books and two CDs in the Grand People's Study House.

IF YOU KNEW TIME AS WELL AS I DO, SAID THE HATTER, *YOU WOULDN'T TALK ABOUT WASTING IT. IT'S HIM.*

LEWIS CARROLL

Alice's Adventures in Wonderland

CHAPTER THIRTEEN

GO GREEN GO

It was late in the day on Sunday when Older Handler gave me the news. My Monday-morning visit to the apogee of Great Leader love, the Kumsusan Palace—where Kim 1 and Kim 2 are kept on ice in their glass mausoleums/offices, since they're still running things from beyond—had been canceled.

Since, as instructed, I'd brought along a set of fancy clothes for the visit, necessitating me packing an extra pair of shoes, my disappointment was palpable. I was not taking this lying down:

ME: Why is it canceled?

OLDER HANDLER: It's closed.

ME: Why is it closed?

OLDER HANDLER: Yes. It's closed.

Because every hour must have a scheduled activity, lest you forget how fabulous Korea is, my NoKo coterie was wasting no time trying to fill the next morning's now vacant 9:00 a.m. to 10:00 a.m. slot.

Older Handler proffered one lame substitution after another, but I am monumented out. I've seen so many American Imperialist exhibits over the past five days, I'm starting to actually believe some of it. So when she hesitantly spat out "football match?" (*football* meaning *soccer*, as opposed to American football), I instantly chirped "football match!" in violent agreement.

She shot me a desperate, pleading look that said, "I beg you not to choose football match," while concurrently asking aloud, "Are you sure? Are you sure?"

I actually felt a tinge of guilt. But yes. I'm sure. And by the way, please modify the schedule so I can stay for the whole match.

A flurry of phone calls—DISCUSSIONS—took place before Older Handler delivered the great news: There just happens to be a professional football match scheduled for just the time I need it: Monday morning at 9:00 a.m. How lucky!

Arriving at nine on the dot (no traffic! never late!), we drove through the empty parking lot of the Kim Il-sung Stadium, the 50,000-seat home of NoKo's national football team and former site of the Arirang Mass Games (a spectacularly-synchronized spectacle with over 100,000 participants, held annually) before the Rungrado May Day Stadium was built. Driver pulled the car curbside in front of the VIP entrance and parked.

I was brought to a room with no lights on and left waiting next to an escalator (which was of course turned off, since everything that can be turned on in NoKo isn't) while my handlers and the stadium staff who'd just greeted us walked up a short flight of stairs and commenced DISCUSSIONS.

After ten minutes or so, my handlers returned to where Driver and I stood waiting, accompanied by the required local guides, an escalator operator, and my ticket to the game. The escalator operator walked over to the VIP escalator and turned it on, but no dice; it wasn't moving. My cabal stood frozen, all smiles, as they considered the urgent need for further DISCUSSIONS. After another five minutes of everyone standing around pretending nothing was wrong while the escalator operator frantically scrambled to get the escalator moving, I asked why we couldn't just walk up the (at most) fifteen escalator stairs? Frozen-tight smile-nods all around.

To my great relief—since I couldn't stand his embarrassment—the escalator operator finally nudged the escalator on, and we rode to the top, which took all of about four seconds…well worth the twenty-five-minute wait. When we reached the top, he promptly turned the escalator off.

As we walked through the corridor and out into the muted salmon-pink and mint-green stadium, Older Handler apologetically explained there wouldn't be many local people there watching because it was 9:00 a.m. on a Monday morning, so "local people are working."

For once she was telling the truth: There were not many local people there. I counted about forty.

As I was escorted through the empty stadium to my VIP seat—a folding chair that had seen better days—the rival teams, River Amrok (in green uniforms) and Light Industry (in white uniforms) had already taken the field and begun to play.

I chose to root for River Amrok; my handlers chose to root for Light Industry. And although few in numbers, the paltry crowd made a valiant attempt at cheering, although for whom, I could not tell.

Fresh Handler seemed genuinely enthralled by the match, shrieking when my team scored and when hers did not (earning a spot on my "Shit I Think Might Be Real" list). I taught her how to smack talk, so we spent the match alternating between calling one another "loo-hoo-sa-her" (holding up an L-shape hand) and telling each other to suck it, whenever our chosen team scored.

Older Handler slept through most of the match. I guess football just wasn't her thing. Coincidentally she woke up once at the exact moment her team had just lost an easy goal and without missing a beat shouted, with pitch-perfect delivery, "Dammit!"

"Did you just say dammit?" I asked, spinning around to face her. I was so shocked, you could have scraped me up off the floor. It was a real reaction (probably to realizing she'd been asleep on the job), for which I'd never loved (*read*: sort of liked) her more; this moment, too, joined my "Shit I Think Might Be Real" list.

A military general sharing our VIP area castigated his team from the stands whenever players made mistakes. He was sitting with one foot resting on his opposite thigh, pants rolled up to his knees, revealing white tube socks that didn't quite go with the rest of his uniform. After one particularly bad play, he took off his hat and cast it aside. I tried to catch his eye since we both seemed to be rooting for the team in green, but he wouldn't make eye contact with me no matter how long I stared.

A lone cameraman was nearby in the stands. I spent a few minutes ruminating on what year his camera was manufactured, and whether he was actually recording or broadcasting anything. Answer: the year cameras were invented, and no.

Then during the second half of the game, like a downpour on a sunny day, a crowd suddenly materialized. A swarm of several hundred people marched in NoKo style—in close formation, in lines of five or six people across and as many deep, and all dressed in military or other uniforms or matching outfits so chronologically out of place they seemed like costumes—and took their seats. I noticed most were watching me instead of the match, as confounded by my presence as I was by their arrival.

Maybe all the local people were suddenly allowed to leave work. Or maybe all those earlier DISCUSSIONS had paid off, and the powers that be realized that a "regularly scheduled" 9 a.m. Monday-morning football match would be more convincing if there were actual fans in the stands. As usual, I had no idea.

In yet another day that will live in infamy for the American Imperialists, the team I was rooting for won.

So was this a real, previously scheduled, Monday-morning-at-9:00-a.m. football match? And had I just been super lucky to have a Monday-morning-at-9:00-a.m. slot on my schedule that needed filling? Possibly, given the damned good luck (knock wood) and propensity for remarkable coincidences I tend to have.

Or had a country just pulled together an entire football match (minus a few thousand fans) in less than twelve hours solely for my benefit? It was a thought too absurd, too egomaniacal, too lunatic, and too paranoid, to even consider…right?

That's the paradox that is North Korea. It's unfathomable that a country without electricity (among other things) could orchestrate a scene this way. But at the same time, the people basically belong to the government/Party, so it's also completely feasible that some higher-up could just say, "You five thousand hoi polloi, come to the stadium now: We need a crowd to form."

ALICE HAD NO IDEA WHAT LATITUDE WAS,
OR LONGITUDE EITHER, BUT THOUGHT THEY
WERE NICE GRAND WORDS TO SAY.

LEWIS CARROLL

Alice's Adventures in Wonderland

CHAPTER FOURTEEN

"SAY CHEESE"

The local guide, whom I've mistaken for a general for some reason, is explaining the "history" of the Korean War. His story is as follows: the American Imperialists started it, the American Imperialists lost it, the American Imperialists were so embarrassed they lost that they forgot their flag. Or something like that.

It hardly matters anyway. It's not accurate, and besides, all I can think to myself is, "He's cute. I wonder if he's single. I should try to fix him up with Fresh Handler."

I'm at the Korean Demilitarized Zone, or DMZ, the swath of land that has divided North from South Korea at the Thirty-Eighth Parallel since the signing of the armistice agreement in 1953. And while I don't doubt that, as the most heavily militarized border in the world, it's inherently dangerous (since the two countries are technically still at war with one another), I am having a little trouble taking the whole thing too seriously when there are posters for sale in the gift shop that look like this:

As someone seriously disinclined to take anything too seriously, particularly things I should probably take seriously, I try hard to stifle my laugher while a gaggle of military soldiers and my handlers go batshit when I accidentally walk to the right of some stanchion instead of the left of it, as we walk from the gift shop to the car that will take us to the actual border. It's made all the more funny—to me at least—when I'm forced to retrace my steps on the offending side, just so I can walk the same five feet, only two feet over to the left.

I'm off to a great start.

My handlers, the aforementioned Non-General, some other soldiers, and I get into one car, while a couple of other soldiers get into cars in front of and behind us. That *is* an awful lot of soldiers. And everyone's so serious. Maybe this place *is* dangerous? But how dangerous could it be when all the soldiers are wearing the same giant, upside-down salad bowls for helmets that they were sporting during the Korean War?

As usual, I am stuck in a self-inflicted, mental-sinkhole-generated maelstrom of doubt, surrounded by so much pomp and circumstance, and so little substance.

Unless...it's the other way around?

As my DMZ phalanx and I begin the three-mile drive south from the gift shop to the literal Thirty-Eighth Parallel, some kind of flying North Korean insect—which heretofore had lain dormant in the fake flowers and vines decorating the inside of the back window—began violently buzzing around the car in what felt like a concerted effort to kill one of us. Neither Older Handler nor any of the soldiers even flinch. Fresh Handler and I, on the other hand, both scream. Arguably, our overwrought reaction to what was probably a big fly is a bit disproportionate, particularly when we are (supposedly) in one of the world's most dangerous places. But that still didn't stop me for one minute from asking if they'd pull the car over to shoo it out.

The look of disbelief crossed with annoyance on Older Handler's face was priceless and immediately earned a spot on my "Shit I Think Might Be Real" list. Needless to say they did not pull the car over.

Older Handler resumes propaganda-talking at me (a new verb I have, by now, invented and adopted into my vocabulary, then quickly shortened to the more affectionate *proptalking*). She's saying something about how the American Imperialists have filled the three-mile zone on their side of the Thirty-Eighth Parallel with weapons and bombs and all things bad, while on North Korea's side exists "nothing for war, only the beautiful farmland," she dreamily tells me.

This, she prattles on, "is because when our Great, Kind, Eternal Leader, who is our Sun and our Father, visited here, he told us he cared more about his people than about weapons, so he gave us advice about how to have the farmland for the growing of food. You see village?"

As usual, I quite literally have no idea what she is talking about. But this is turning out to be one of the greatest days of my life.

Our next stop is a small wooden stand-alone building, painted white on the inside, with low-hung blue windows where walls should be. It's so quiet, calm, peaceful, and full of natural light, I start feeling as if there is an

inverse ratio between proximity to the Thirty-Eighth Parallel and danger. Inside, Non-General explains the history of the room as Fresh Handler translates. Older Handler calls all the shots, including who gets to translate for me when, and it's Fresh Handler's turn.

Fresh Handler is somewhat lacking as a translator. Her English is good enough, but she's exceedingly nervous and doesn't trust herself, so she's convinced she's making mistakes even when she's not. But I really like her. She truly seems sweet. And on the North Korean scale of cuckoo-for-Cocoa-Puffs bullshit—with crazy, ignoramus cult member rating a ten, and *The Truman Show's* Truman Burbank realizing his entire life has been a giant lie a one—I'm guessing Fresh Handler is a solid five. I often think to myself that turning her would be pretty easy, were we not in a country where extraction was anything more than a pipe dream.

So whenever it's her turn, I try to listen encouragingly, smiling and nodding along as she speaks, doing my best to focus on what she's saying. But it's really no use. Garbage in, garbage out, as the saying goes, and instead I soon find myself focusing on trying to telepathically communicate everything I want her to know but can't say: Your country's a sham, and your Great Dear dead Leaders are neither the sun nor god, nor can they rule your country from their graves; and the only genius advice any of them are providing during their on-the-spot-guidance visits is how to point.

As she stands there proptalking and I stand there trying to listen, I feel an overwhelming need to comfort her and tell her it's okay. That she needn't try so hard. Older Handler is outside flirting with some military guy, and I don't care.

When my posse exits the building for our next stop, I ask if I can take a

186

few more photos of the room before I leave. Instead I sneak a photo of nice Non-General and a man I can't identify, who exit before me. The man has his hands crossed behind his back, and for a few seconds Non-General takes his arm. It looks like Non-General has arrested the man and is carting him off to jail. I'm saddened by the irony...since, for all intents and purposes, the man's already there.

I catch up to the others as we enter the Peace Museum, where the armistice agreement was signed. Non-General tells me the American Imperialists had wanted to sign the agreement in a tent, but the Great Supreme Leader insisted it be signed in a building, so there'd be a permanent monument to the NoKo victory over the United States. Non-General says the North Koreans managed to build the building the night before (of course) and something about the American Imperialists being so ashamed by their humiliating loss at the hands of the Great Supreme Leader that they got down on their knees and apologized before rushing from the room and forgetting their flag (or something like that), and some equally cockamamy explanation for why the U.N. flag is a shambles, while the NoKo flag is almost perfectly preserved.

I trust my gut implicitly, and I'm a good judge of character, so I just can't reconcile what's coming out of Non-General's mouth with the intelligent, kind, and genuine man he seems to be. Does he really believe the stories he's telling me? It's as if the U.S. president took to the airwaves one day to warn us that apples and oranges have finally reached common ground and are staging a coup...and meant it. I'm confounded.

The retelling of history retold, our motorcade proceeds south to the Thirty-Eighth Parallel, where we pull into a sizeable parking lot—which is, of course, devoid of cars. We walk down a small slope and around a corner, past a monument with a copy of Kim Il-sung's final signature (he died the next day). The local guide stops us so we can stare at the copy of his signature on a rock for a few minutes, in deference to the Dear Great Supreme Leader, because that's what you do in NoKo.

Older Handler breaks the silence by saying something about NoKo's flagpole being taller than SoKo's flagpole, in a tone so boastful it sounds like "nah nah nah nah nah nah," while directing my attention to one flagpole then the other. Good god, I think to myself, if we're fighting over flagpole height at the DMZ, mankind is doomed, and then shake off the thought as we move on to the main attraction.

Save for the dozen or so NoKo soldiers escorting my gang, the Joint Security Area is a ghost town—as deserted as a suburban office park on a Sunday afternoon. There is no one there, and nothing going on. "Where is everyone?" I ask, my confusion and disappointment palpable, "I thought this would be scarier." No one answers. Ask a stupid question, and everyone just thinks you're an idiot.

One main blue building straddles North and South Korea. Like all other tourists to the DMZ, I enter it from the side I'm on—in my case, the North. Inside, I sit in the translator's seat, my left side in the South, my right side in the North—a stupid, silly border, the source of so much pain death, crossed just like that. North Korean soldiers stared at South Korean soldiers while Fresh Handler snapped photos of me shaking hands across the border with Non-General and I snapped photos of Non-General with his military friends. I'd been told that photographing anyone in the military was strictly forbidden, but for whatever reason, no one at the Thirty-Eighth Parallel seemed to care.

189

Back outside and in North Korea, I have the weirdest sensation of being on the wrong side of the tracks. I feel like a traitor, or a Potemkin trophy being paraded around like a hostage by his or her captors. I ask Fresh Handler what would happen if I made a break for it and ran to the other side.

"They'll shoot you," was all she said.

I wanted a photo of me alone in front of the infamous blue buildings that separate North from South, so I hung back a moment and gave Fresh Handler a chance to snap my photo. The soldiers and other handlers had walked at most three giant steps ahead before noticing I'd fallen eleven seconds behind, which as you can see by the soldier coming to fetch me, was eleven seconds too many. Turns out the DMZ is no joke, even though it felt like one.

Inside the austere Panmungak Hall, the main building on the North Korean side, the lights are all off, so the hallways and stairwells are dim. As in the rest of the DMZ, aside from our group there's not another soul in sight. Maybe everyone's downstairs in a bunker or somewhere in the building out of view, but a bustling intelligence center this is not.

Fresh Handler and I need to use the bathroom. As this is not a scheduled event, it takes them forever to decide which bathroom we should use and then forever again to find the key. The musty-smelling facility reminds me of a junior-high bathroom, only with no lights or running water. As I pass Fresh Handler my hand sanitizer, I ask her if she ever tires of never being able to wash her hands after using the toilet. She makes a face that I've come to understand means, "I cannot say yes," then gratefully applies the gel like an old pro.

As we exit Panmungak Hall and head for our cars, I suddenly remember I've brought my instant camera with me but left it in the car. I often travel with my instant camera, especially to countries where cameras are rare or a luxury. I take many photos of people who so generously pose for me; I love returning the favor by giving them photos of themselves.

I've been using my instant camera as an icebreaker in North Korea. No one has ever seen anything like it before, and each person I photograph stands amazed, staring at the magic of the photo developing right before their eyes. I originally hoped to take two photos of me with each person I met—one for me, and one for the person—as a sort of a bridge-the-divide project. But that's proven impossible, and it's turned out to be much nicer and more fun to just watch the surprise and joy on each person's face as they see themselves appear, without asking for anything in return.

I plead with Older Handler for just a few more minutes so I can retrieve the camera to snap photos for Non-General and a few of the soldiers.

She says okay. She's a big fan of the instant camera.

There's a pervasive sense of nervous energy in the air as I flail around animatedly, trying to explain the mechanics of the instant camera and what I'd like to do, as the uncomprehending crowd of soldiers debates whether to shoot me. For once, Older Handler has nothing to say.

With my life on the line, I implore Older Handler to translate, which she does reluctantly, putting a welcome end to my one-woman show. Since no one seems to know if the taking of instant photos is allowed or not, the soldiers all remain at their assigned posts, and for a minute or two no one moves a muscle.

Non-General, being the stand-up guy I have suspected him to be, bravely makes the first move and steps forward to be photographed. We stand next to each other as he clutches the blank piece of film, waiting for the magic to happen. The smile that breaks across his face as we watch his image come together almost makes me weep. It definitely makes me tear. He shows the photo to the soldiers standing closest to him first and then to more soldiers a few steps away. Their excitement is unmistakable. Words are exchanged from one soldier to the next, and like that, all the soldiers—literally all of them—leave their posts and queue up, waiting for me to say "Say cheese!"

And I thought the poster in the gift shop was going to be the high point of the day.

My surreal visit to the DMZ comes to a close. I'm awash in emotions and conflicting thoughts, and the part of me seriously disinclined to take anything too seriously is not disappointed. After all, I've managed to disarm and distract NoKo's entire DMZ security detail with a $98 instant camera.

193

ALL THIS SHE TOOK IN LIKE A PICTURE...
AND LISTENING, IN A HALF DREAM, TO THE
MELANCHOLY MUSIC OF THE SONG.

LEWIS CARROLL

Through the Looking-Glass

CHAPTER FIFTEEN

THE DAY I HIT THE WALL

I didn't remember selecting "Concrete Wall" from the list I'd been given when choosing activities for my customized itinerary. And a concrete wall certainly didn't sound like something that would normally have piqued my interest (akin to choosing "watch paint dry"). But it was on our agenda for the day after the DMZ, and quite frankly it sounded better than some of the other shit I'd been dragged around to (can you say, Victorious Fatherland Liberation War Museum?), so it felt like a win.

For a minute it seemed like Fresh Handler was trying to talk me out of visiting the Concrete Wall—not that I was dying to visit it, or even had any idea what the Concrete Wall was, aside from the obvious.

FRESH HANDLER: You want go Concrete Wall?

ME: I don't know. What's the Concrete Wall?

FRESH HANDLER: It's a concrete wall.

ME: I don't understand. It's just a concrete wall?

FRESH HANDLER: Yes.

ME: Why would we go look at a concrete wall?

FRESH HANDLER, *giggling, shrugging shoulders while making a face that says, "You got me…I don't know why we'd go look at a concrete wall"*: You can't see wall.

ME: What do you mean we can't see the wall? I don't understand. I thought you said we were going to see a concrete wall?

FRESH HANDLER: Wall is very far. You can't see it. You look at wall through hole.

ME: What do you mean we look at wall through hole?

FRESH HANDLER, *giggling, covering her mouth with her hand while looking to the sky for the right word*: Ahh, wall is very far away. You look through, ahh…

ME: Binoculars?

FRESH HANDLER, *delighted*: Yes! You look through binoculars to see wall. But can't see wall.

Okay, got it. We look through binoculars to see a concrete wall that we can't see. I'm so happy I understand her that I momentarily forget I don't understand her.

ME: So we're going to look at a concrete wall that you can only see through binoculars, but you still can't see it?

FRESH HANDLER, *motioning with her hand to indicate something close to "Yes…I told you this was a stupid idea"*: Sort of.

She looked a little embarrassed.

Sensing that my current line of questioning was likely to end up with Fresh Handler in tears, I changed tack.

"Is it close to where we are now?" We were still at the DMZ.

> **FRESH HANDLER:** Ohhh, nooo. Very far. More than one-hour drive back to Kaesong, and then one-hour drive back to wall. And road is very bumpy. Road not so good.

This was sounding fucking *awesome*.

"So we drive from here all the way back to Kaesong, then we drive another hour on a bad, bumpy road to a concrete wall that we can only see by looking through binoculars? But we can't see it. So what do we see?"

> **FRESH HANDLER:** Just wall.

She smile-giggle-shrugged.

I was in, and we were off. We left the DMZ and drove back to Kaesong.

Somewhere near the center of town, Driver pulled over in front of a small building, and an older gentleman who looked to be in his seventies (hard to tell) and was dressed in a military uniform exited the building, ambled over, and joined us in our car.

There was something about him that made him immediately endearing. Maybe it was the kind look in his eyes or the warmth he emanated. Or maybe it was because he looked so sad-cute in his two-sizes-too-big military uniform that I wanted to squeeze him. It was like he'd shrunk but was stuck wearing the same uniform.

He cordially shook my hand, introduced himself as General So-and-So, and immediately started asking me questions, but not the normal rapid-fire questions almost all North Koreans hit you with in an unfriendly interrogation style immediately upon making your acquaintance: Your first time come Korea? You been to South Korea? You speak Korean? You been to Japan? Where you from?

Instead his questions were sweet, like he really wanted to get to know me: Did I like kimchi? Did I like Korean music? Was I traveling alone? Why was I traveling alone? Did I enjoy traveling alone? Was I ever afraid? Did I read the newspaper?

His gentle line of questioning continued unabated as we serpentined slowly through the countryside toward the Concrete Wall.

What was my job? Did I like my job? Was I good at my job? How many people worked for me? What did I study in school? Where did I live? Did I like where I lived? Was it cold where I lived? What was my favorite thing to do?

In between questions he told me about his daughter and little bits of this and that. Older Handler and Fresh Handler took turns translating, with Fresh Handler filling in the blanks.

Then he started congratulating me, telling Fresh Handler to tell me, "You are very brave woman. Come very dangerous place alone."

Older Handler rolled her eyes upon hearing of my bravery.

We carried on chatting like schoolgirls throughout the ride, with General speaking directly to me whenever Fresh Handler wasn't keeping pace with the translating. Between his genial disposition and his comely looks, chatty General was winning me over big time.

After about an hour we turned onto an unmarked, steep, bumpy road and chugged up bends and turns until we finally reached the summit.

We climbed a flight of stairs to a small, plain building set among trees, fields, rolling hills, and random scrub. It was completely quiet except for a breeze. It was as lonely as I imagined General to be, in the fake, sad life I was inventing for him.

He directed us into a room on the left. We took our seats and watched as he starred in a high-school performance of *The Concrete Wall*. His showmanship was outstanding. He tapped and pointed and gesticulated until he could gesticulate no more as he solemnly explained (in the male version of the urgent, hushed-whisper voice that all local guides employ) everything about said Wall:

In the late 1970s, at the behest of the American Imperialists (he looked at me apologetically while uttering this phrase), the South Koreans built a concrete wall along the entire length of the DMZ. The wall is sixteen-and-a-half to twenty-six feet tall at various points, as thick as sixty-two feet at the bottom, and as wide as twenty-three feet at the top, or the other way around—it wasn't completely clear since Fresh Handler was translating. And for some reason the Wall is invisible from South Korea. This part wasn't completely clear either, but not because of Fresh Handler's translation skills. Rather because the explanation didn't make any sense.

At the top of Act Two, it occurred to me how strange it is that I've never heard about this Wall before. I mean, I'd heard more about the Wall on *Game of Thrones*, and I've missed half the episodes. Wouldn't the Korean Wall have come up at some point in history—say when the Berlin Wall was coming down?

But since General was now my boyfriend, I felt like I had to support him, even if he was asserting that the Wall was an "American Imperialist belt (again, he apologized with his eyes) cinched around Korea's waist" (or something like that—Fresh Handler again translating) or that it was a symbol that the American Imperialists (sorry eyes again) "don't want the reunification of our country." And he looked so lonely in his big-people clothes. So I zipped it and carried on watching the show.

When he was done we stepped outside onto the patio (a.k.a., the very serious viewing deck), along the perimeter of which were four or five binoculars attached to poles. The binoculars had to be 700 years old. And they were all scratched up. One pair was worse than the next.

General spent a few minutes concentrating, staring intently through a pair, adjusting, and adjusting a bit more until he aimed the binoculars just so. Then he called me over to look through. He pointed in the direction of the binoculars, toward the horizon, and said, in English, "Wall."

I stared, and I stared, and then I stared some more. Fresh Handler was right. I was looking through a hole, at a wall I couldn't see.

I didn't want to hurt General's feelings, so I blamed myself. "My eyes are really bad," I said apologetically. Or, I thought to myself, maybe you could spring for some better binoculars so there's a fighting chance we can see the thing. But I was still giving General the benefit of the doubt then.

He moved on to the next pair of binoculars and labored over setting that pair up, too. I stared again and thought I saw something that could have been a wall (wishful seeing?), but it was too far away and so incredibly small; there was just no way to tell.

When I looked through the third pair of binoculars he'd carefully pointed south, I was taken aback when I looked through the hole and saw a large South Korean military post filled with soldiers staring back at me.

I was riveted. Holy cow! I could literally see the soldiers, down to what they were wearing and doing. Of course this meant they could see me. Only they could actually see me, because I'm guessing they had way better binoculars on the South side.

Could they tell I was American? Did they know I was the same traitor from back at the DMZ? Should I wave? Hold up a sign that says, "Hey, down there, in case you're wondering…it sucks up here"?

For every one aged general we had on our side, they had…umm… at least forty-five soldiers, with guns, doing soldier stuff, in a modern, glass, X-shape building that looked white on the outside and blue on the inside (probably just the binoculars breaking light), with all kinds of towers and things poking out of it, and computer screens, and chairs. *And* they had a highway on their side, with cars!

As if we'd grown so close he could read my mind, Boyfriend General said to Fresh Handler, who said to me, "He praises you for your courage and said he will shield you from any stray bullets from the South."

With that, Older Handler turned heel and walked back into the building, while I died of laughter on the inside.

"Thank you. Please tell him thank you. I feel much safer now. That's very nice." (Does he know there's no wall? Wait, there *is* no wall, right? What if there is no wall, and he knows there is no wall—can I still love him? What if he thinks there's a wall, and there is no wall? Then there's something wrong with him. Then I'll feel so sad for him, I'll do anything to help. But maybe that's why he's so endearing in the first place—he must ingratiate himself with tourists. How the fuck else is he going to sell us this wall?)

Luckily he broke into song, cutting short my *petitio principii*.

When he finished singing (just a few bars, but you could definitely tell why he'd won the lead role in this one-man play), Fresh Handler told me I could take photos with him on the grass, so I did. I was thinking how ironic it was that one of the friendliest people I'd met during my trip was a general.

We drove back to Kaesong in the same configuration, and General resumed his questioning from before. How many countries had I been to? Which ones were my favorites? Which ones did I want to go back to? Would I come back to visit Korea some time?

When we returned to the spot where we had met General earlier, Driver pulled the car over for him to get out. But this time all five of us got out of the car.

I attach to people quickly, but compartmentally and situationally. It's a little hard to explain, but it's why I can be standing in front of General and in the moment be profoundly sad (like in tears) saying good-bye, while at the exact same time not give a shit if I ever see him again.

So I stood in front of him, and we shook hands, and I told him how glad I was to have met him. I wanted so badly to exchange names and email addresses, the way I've done hundreds of times, with hundreds of people, in tons of countries.

But this was North Korea.

He told Fresh Handler to tell me I was a brave woman one last time, then gave me a big grin good-bye.

The remaining cast members and I got back into the car and headed toward Pyongyang. As one does, after a lovely day, I remembered aloud some of the finer points of my afternoon and mentioned General's serenade as a top one.

Older Handler threw her fingers back dismissively while making a *pish* sound. Then, her face as expressionless as a cat's, she said, "Oh, he sings to all the girls. They call him Karaoke General."

I don't know if she was being spiteful for all of our normal girlfriend drama, or because she'd sensed I liked General more than her, but I wasn't going to let her see me bothered by this.

"Hmm," I grin-grunted in silent acknowledgment. "That's so nice of him."

I was dying inside again—but this time from sadness. My worst fears had been confirmed: even cute, disheveled, affable, sweet Boyfriend General is not to be trusted. He sings for all the girls.

I may or may not have visited a wall that may or may not exist. Fresh Handler may or may not have known it exists, and may or may not have been trying to let me know this. General may be senile, or may be sly as a fox, or may be under the threat of death if he doesn't meet some arbitrary quota of "I Saw the Wall" team converts. Had he been genuinely nice, or was he just vying for my vote?

I'd hit the wall…again.

Despite my best efforts to hide my dismay, Older Handler must have noticed my consternation, because she looked at me and said, "You're not tired are you? We go to Funfair next!"

I'VE A RIGHT TO THINK, SAID ALICE SHARPLY, FOR SHE WAS BEGINNING TO FEEL A LITTLE WORRIED.

LEWIS CARROLL

Alice's Adventures in Wonderland

CHAPTER SIXTEEN

MY MIND IS A TERRIBLE THING TO WASTE

F iguring out whether intelligence tradecraft was being employed against tourists like me or not—and if so, to what extent—was like most everything else in NoKo: endless fodder for mental masturbation.

You are warned unequivocally not to bring anything into North Korea that can be misconstrued as anti-NoKo or anti-Great Leader. But beyond the obvious (e.g., a book about why North Korea sucks), discerning what constitutes *anti* is not easy. In the wake of American (Imperialist) tourist Jeffrey Fowle being arrested and detained (and thankfully since released) for having left a Bible in a "nightclub" bathroom only two months before my arrival, I tended to err on the side of caution, as clearly leave-behinds can be misconstrued.

Thus, for example, when I grew tired of carrying around a slim Korean phrase book, I thought twice about throwing it in a trash bin, lest a maid find it and turn it over to the real or imagined tourist Gestapo, and next thing you know I'm waiting for Bill Clinton to negotiate my release. So instead I ripped the book into a million pieces (thankfully, it was a soft cover) and flushed it down the toilet in the bathroom in my hotel room.

I'm satisfied with a job well done. I also feel like a complete jackass for being so paranoid.

I'm highly mindful and operate in a constant state of heightened awareness. I naturally pay close attention to everything going on around me and am overly sensitive to others' emotional states and nonverbal clues. I know where my thoughts and emotions are taking me, and if I need to or want to, how to consciously adjust my behavior, personality, speech—really anything or everything, as a result. So, while not ideal, being watched wasn't entirely upsetting to me. But my unrelenting dissatisfaction over never knowing what was really going on *was*.

I'd purchased a tote bag in the "gift shop" at the Grand People's Study House on a lark. It was the same nylon-blend material and sky-blue color as those original Pan Am cabin bags the Jet Set carried on board in the 1960s, only this one said, "See you back in Pyongyang." It struck me as funny at the time I bought it, and I imagined myself chuckling when using it after returning home. But days later, while sitting in my hotel room near Mount Myohyang during another particularly trying "I can't stand NoKo" kind of day, the thought of having to cart around the now offensive memento one minute longer (let alone schlepp it back and use it in New York City) had become mighty hard to stomach.

I knew I was being irrational, so I tried reasoning with myself: "While I highly doubt there's any law or case to be made against you for leaving a newly purchased pro-Pyongyang carryon bag behind—in fact, they may even appreciate it—why take chances? You are leaving NoKo in two-and-a-half days (!!!), and it's not like you haven't been carrying the stupid bag around for the past few days, anyway. The tote bag weighs nothing, and you don't even notice it in the outside pocket of your suitcase. So just be smart, and suck it up, and put the tote bag back in your suitcase. You can throw the thing away as soon as you land in Beijing. *Ça va?*"

Non. Instead, I "hid" the bag in plain sight on the far side of the unused twin bed in my room. I reasoned that by putting it there, no one would see it if they quickly eyeballed the room after I'd vacated, but when found, it would look like it had accidentally fallen on the floor when I was reorganizing my suitcase or something, versus my shoving it under the bed or someplace similar where it would look like I'd been trying to purposely hide it.

I don't know if my small act of rebellion against my inner voice of reason was a triumph over paranoia run amok, or proof that being self aware does not always mean you choose to forgo kowtowing to exceedingly illogical thoughts or emotions (like not being able to stand the sight of something one second longer, even when you know you won't be able to even see the dumb thing once it's packed in your suitcase, but you'll still know it's there…). It was probably a little of both. But there was no way "See you back in Pyongyang" was leaving Mount Myohyang.

The next morning in the parking lot, Driver, Fresh Handler, and I loaded up our car to leave, but Older Handler was nowhere to be seen. When she finally emerged from the hotel, she made a beeline for me, "Do you have everything?" A normal question, sure, but one she'd never asked me before.

"Yup. Sure do," I answered confidently, having nearly convinced myself it was the truth.

She pushed me again, "Are you sure?"

"Yes. I'm sure." I was steadfast. I would not be brought down by a Pan Am knockoff.

"You looked everywhere? Nothing in room?" She entreated (I hoped) one last time.

I was more resolute now than ever. I had a story to stick to. "Yes, I am sure I have everything." My fate was now sealed, although in which direction, I was not sure.

As we stood staring at each other for a beat, a woman who worked at the hotel came running outside, calling loudly for Older Handler, who turned and walked back to where the employee was standing. DIS-CUSSIONS ensued.

Shit, I thought to myself. This probably isn't good.

At that moment, the same part of my brain that thought it was a good idea to spend fifteen minutes tearing a phrase book to shreds before flushing it down a toilet was wondering why it hadn't thought to do the same with the fucking tote bag. Please, I thought to myself, let's all just get in the car and go.

I smile at Fresh Handler and make the universal "what the what" face, while asking her out loud what's going on. Because we've become pals by now (at least when Older Handler isn't paying attention) and she's feeling invested in my well-being (as I am in hers), she's also become my de facto bellwether of sorts, her facial expressions and reactions letting me know what's to come. But her double shoulder shrug says simply, "I don't know," so we join Driver in the car and wait.

Whether leaving my Pyongyang-purchased bag behind was a no-no or not, I'll never know. Once DISCUSSIONS were concluded, Older Handler returned to the car, taking her seat next to me. Handing me two U.S. one-dollar bills, she says merely, "Your change." Seems there was a miscalculation over the number of water bottles I'd purchased the night before, and the hotel's restaurant staff had charged me more than the amount that was due—or something like that.

"Thanks," I replied and let out a deep breath, as Driver started the car, and once again I felt like a paranoid fool.

I take some solace knowing NoKo induces similar delusions in other tourists. One afternoon while picnicking in the Sariwon Folk Village, we encounter a family of four visiting from Australia. Of course our respective handlers never leave our sides. So after we introduce ourselves and exchange the normal, non-trouble-inducing pleasantries (Did you fly from Beijing? What cities are you visiting? What hotel did you stay in?), our eleven-second-long "free association" conversation goes like this:

ME: So how do you like Korea?

THEM, *fake smiles, imploring eyes*: It's great! How are you finding Korea?

ME, *fake smile, imploring eyes*: Oh, me too. Great! I'm learning so much. Aren't you?

THEM, *subtle sarcasm evident to us five only, we hope*: Oh yes! So much.

ME, *also employing nuanced sarcasm*: Ten days was really the perfect amount of time to really get to see the country.

THEM: Wow! Ten whole days...you don't say. That is a fine amount of time.

ME: Indeed.

Help me.

And...scene.

Even though my handlers monitored every movement I made and conversation I had, I guess I never seriously considered that my hotel rooms might be bugged. I mean I did, but because I was alone in my room and therefore not speaking out loud, and because I couldn't make any outside calls, and there's no internet, and they knew what was on TV, and they'd searched me for any electronics at the airport when I'd landed and knew I had no computer or other communication devices, I'd more or less dismissed the thought. Why would they bother?

I was barely in my room anyway, and when I was I did little more than sleep or read or get dressed or undressed, or if in Room 2-10-28 at the Hotel Koryo, watch the BBC.

Except for that one afternoon.

After I refused to visit the Sinchon Museum of American War Atrocities, we'd arrived back in Pyongyang earlier than expected. Older Handler did her best to reconfigure our itinerary, but our next activity—"Enjoy draft beer at Paradise Bar"—was less fun than expected. We were the only patrons in the dark, freezing establishment, and my crew was riveted to the tiny television hung high above and behind me that was showing a Chinese drama with Korean subtitles that apparently they all loved. When their show concluded, I asked if we could go back to the hotel. "More people at night," Older Handler assured me. *Whatever*, I didn't say, and we rolled.

Ensconced back in my by-now-it's-so-familiar-it-almost-feels-like-home-except-I'd-kill-myself-if-it-was room at the Koryo, I'm lying on my bed, slightly buzzed, with an unexpected and glorious hour *all to myself, during the daytime*, to kill. I don't feel like watching the BBC, or reading, or learning more vocabulary words, so I take a seat in my room's "lounge" to stare outside. I'm putting my earphones in to listen to music on my iPhone when it strikes me for the first time since arriving in NoKo that if I take my earphones off, I can play music *aloud.*

I couldn't believe I hadn't thought of this sooner!

And even better...I'll do yoga! I haven't exercised since arriving. No wonder I'm so sad. And yoga will be good for me. My mind could use a break.

I didn't bring workout clothes with me, so I strip down to my bra and underpants. I select the yoga mix I've created, prop my iPhone up against the wall, hit Play (careful it's not too loud), and start Downward Dogging my way to bliss. But I'm not even halfway through my first Sun Salutation when the door to my room bangs open, and someone—perhaps a maid—bursts in.

Huh...maybe my room *is* bugged?

Or...? Who fucking knows?

I jump up, staring at her with my mouth agape. Momentarily befuddled, I have no idea what to say. "I'm exercising," I somehow manage. "Is the music too loud?" But I know full well I'm the only one on my floor to hear it.

She'd walked in on me while I was more or less naked, folded over in a V. So unless she's familiar with yoga, or was, in the moments leading up to this intrusion, *SPYING*, she must be as flummoxed as I. She says something I don't quite catch and leaves my room, closing the door behind her. I'm left wondering—among other things, of course—how she even got my door open so quickly, when I can barely open it half the time using my key.

I'm tempted to keep practicing yoga, if for no other reason than to see what "they'll" do, but I'm tired—nay, exhausted—from all my double thinking. Inner peace in the presence of the omnipresent Dear Great dead Leaders, it seems, is simply not possible...for me at least.

Nevertheless I allow myself one millisecond to think that indeed, if I'm not being paranoid, then "they" have just let it be known: As a guest in their country, yoga's just one more thing I'm not allowed to do. And with that, I turn off the music, put my clothes back on, and resume staring outside.

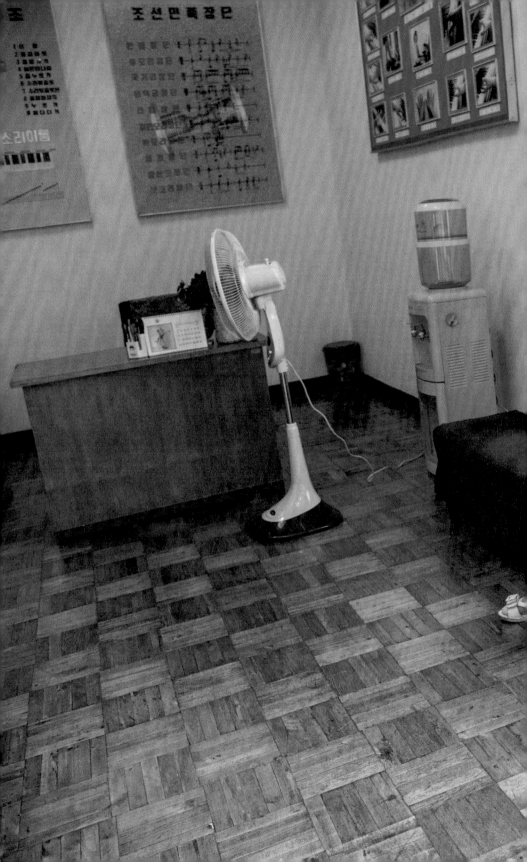

MAYBE IT'S ALWAYS PEPPER THAT MAKES PEOPLE HOT-TEMPERED, SHE WENT ON, VERY MUCH PLEASED AT HAVING FOUND OUT A NEW KIND OF RULE, *AND VINEGAR THAT MAKES THEM SOUR— AND CAMOMILE THAT MAKES THEM BITTER—*

LEWIS CARROLL

Alice's Adventures in Wonderland

CHAPTER SEVENTEEN

THE OLDER ONE

My scheduled activity for the hour was "Moranbong Park to mingle with local people/take photos." My itinerary literally said "mingle with local people," meaning any people whose job was not directly or indirectly related to my tour.

That's how rare it is for visitors to NoKo to speak with local people—and how much they know you want to: they put it on your itinerary as an *actual activity*. The thing is, that, too, is a farce. There's no mingling with local people, at least not in the way you or I mingle. When you see local people, you mainly just get to acknowledge one another, like you do with animals in a zoo. It was disappointing and frustrating.

Fresh Handler had gone to find a bathroom, so I was alone with Older Handler for the first time since arriving—even though it was my second-to-last day there. It was hot as we trudged up the long hill to reach the park entrance, and I could see that she was dragging behind me, struggling to keep up. I knew that if I got too far ahead of her, there in the middle of Pyongyang where others could bear witness, it would reflect poorly on her, so I slowed my pace. I didn't want her to get in trouble. We'd been together forever by then, and because I was leaving so soon, I was feeling a strange mix of wistfulness, frustration and empathy.

When we reached the top of the first hill, we climbed a set of stairs, then turned to the right to climb another set of stairs to reach the main viewing pavilion at the top. There was a group of art students casually sitting on and around the stairs, painting, as if it was the most natural thing in the world for a bunch of North Koreans to just be hanging around doing art on a Wednesday morning. And maybe it was; I didn't know anymore, and I didn't bother asking, since I'd decided by then that Older Handler was incapable of telling the truth.

Older Handler was actually younger than me, but her demeanor and disposition told a different story. She was pushy, and strict about rules, and her beatific smile and overbearing solicitousness did little to conceal her special kind of crazy. When she wasn't literally poking me, she was asking me how much I liked Korea, to which I'd answer (more often as the week wore on), "about as much as I did the last time you asked me." We had a vexed relationship, to say the least.

We continued along to the viewing pavilion, and after taking in the view of Pyongyang below, I asked if we could just sit. She was perplexed, "Sit?" I clarified, "I'd like to just sit outside and enjoy being outdoors without actually having to do anything. You know, *relax*. Can't we just sit here for a few minutes and enjoy the sun, and each other's company?" After all, we'd been dragging around nonstop from early in the morning until after dinner, usually visiting eight to ten places a day, for what felt like, by then, my entire adult life.

Maybe she was tired of all the dragging around, too, because she agreed— and so we sat. There weren't any benches to sit on, since I guess no one just sits around relaxing in the park, except for old people, who weren't so much relaxing as they were waiting to die (so Older Handler intimated). So we sat on the ground next to each other and "relaxed."

As we relaxed, I asked Older Handler if I could take photos of the old people we'd seen in the park, taking in the sun (while waiting to die).

OLDER HANDLER: No.

I asked Older Handler why not.

OLDER HANDLER: To be honest, the old people. They old-thinking. They don't like Americans.

ME: Okay then. I am American.

Next hundreds of Young Pioneers on a field trip swarmed around us. You see huge groups of children everywhere you go in NoKo; my handlers told me they constitute thirty percent of the population. In most cases all but the bravest ignore you. Like everyone else in NoKo, they're scared to talk to you for fear of being killed, or at the very least getting in trouble. And/or they hate you because they've been taught since birth to believe that you, a foreigner—worse, an American Imperialist—are at the root of all evil in their country. I always felt proud of the children who stopped to stare at me—the brave ones, whose innate curiosity or skepticism trumped their fear. Stopping to stare, and in some cases say hello, may sound trivial, but in NoKo, it made them game changers.

Our unscheduled stop was threatening to throw us off our omnipresent and unforgiving schedule, and I could see Older Handler getting nervous about this. I appreciated her having stopped for my benefit, and I felt like we were finally starting to bond a little where we hadn't before, so I asked if she was ready to keep walking.

As we walked through the park, we passed a group of local people playing some kind of game. I asked if I could take a photograph. She hastily replied no.

We carried on walking. A few minutes later she stopped, touched my arm, and began explaining how she used to be a "businesswoman" before becoming a tour guide and that she longed to be one again. She then told me she wanted to open a coffee shop and asked if I would be her business partner.

In addition to being just plain shocked, I couldn't think of anything I wanted to do less. I hated North Korea, couldn't wait to leave, didn't particularly like her, and I was pretty sure some tour guide couldn't just up and decide to switch jobs one day to open a coffee shop with the help of an American Imperialist. Besides, what would be the point? From what I'd seen, it certainly didn't appear as if anyone had any extra money, or free time, or drank coffee, with the possible exception of the art kids hanging out on the stairs.

"Sure," I said. "That sounds great. I'd be happy to help you." And in the strangest way, I wish I could have.

Her phone rang. It was Fresh Handler, whom I'd briefly forgotten about. She was lost somewhere in the park. She'd been wandering around trying to find the pavilion the entire time we'd been there and had finally given up and was calling for help. I guess the only "local" people familiar with the park were old people, Young Pioneers, art students, and handlers who weren't fresh. Or maybe she just had a terrible sense of direction.

Older Handler gave Fresh Handler directions to reach the landmark Moranbong Theater at the edge of the park, as we changed course to go meet her.

YOU OUGHT TO BE ASHAMED OF YOURSELF

FOR ASKING SUCH A SIMPLE QUESTION...

LEWIS CARROLL

Alice's Adventures in Wonderland

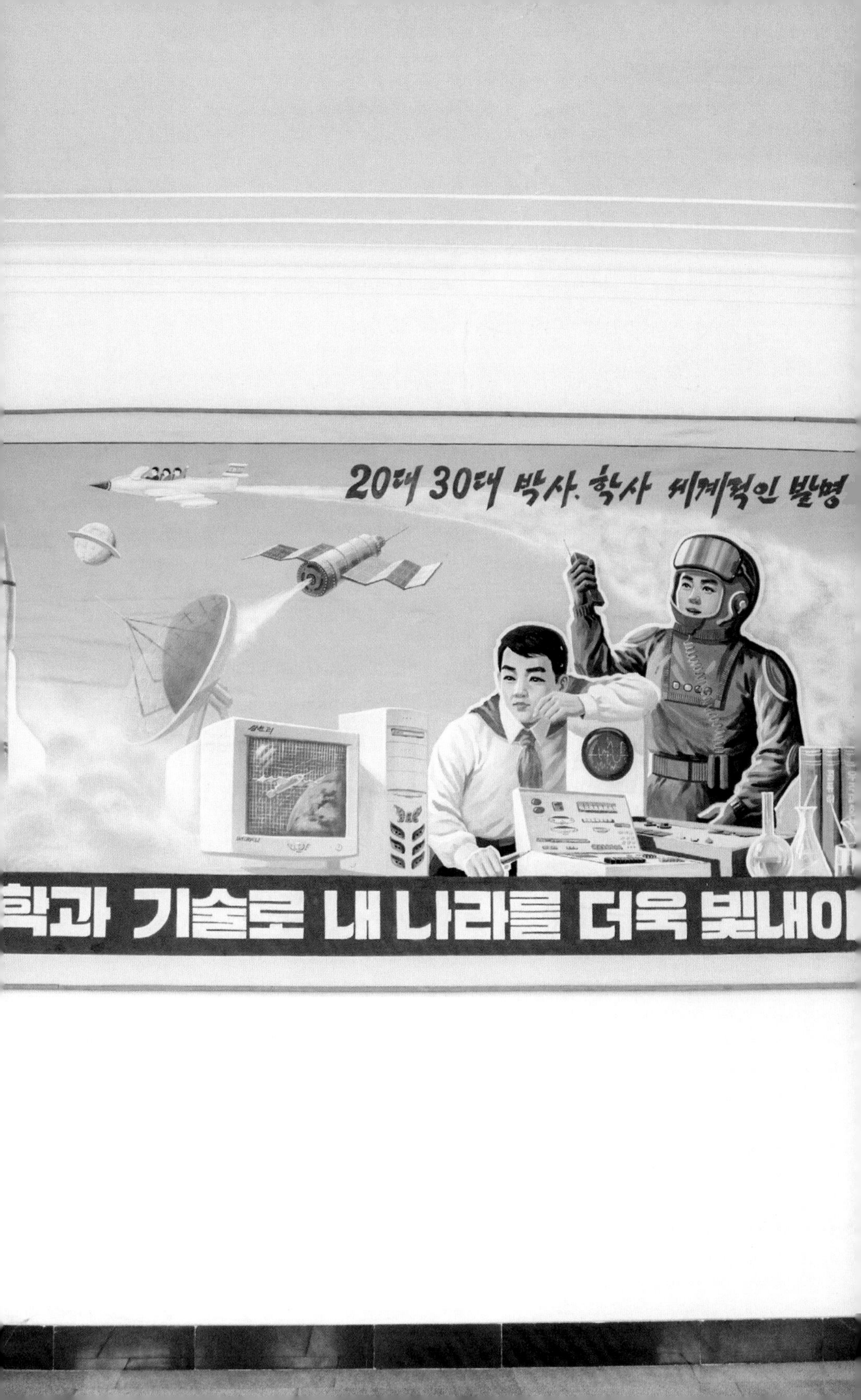
20대 30대 박사. 학사 세계적인 발명
학과 기술로 내 나라를 더욱 빛내이

CHAPTER EIGHTEEN

AND THE EARTH GOES 'ROUND THE SUN

O n my second-to-last day in NoKo, I was taken to Pyongyang's answer to Washington DC's Smithsonian, the Three Rivers Exhibition.

The Three Rivers Exhibition details the "three revolutions: ideological, technical, and cultural" accomplished by the Supreme Great Leader in postwar Korea.

This translates to a sprawling, drab campus comprised of six different architecturally uninspired buildings. The only exception was the planetarium, which I think is shaped like Saturn minus two rings, or Earth plus one ring. Each purportedly showcased Korea's respective advances in technology, manufacturing, heavy industry, light industry, agriculture, or electronics.

As we strolled through the empty, dimly lit, freezing-cold, enormous hall showcasing light industry, I felt like a character on the TV show *Lost* who had just discovered the camp where the Others lived.

Glass case after glass case meant to showcase Korea's engineering and manufacturing prowess displayed objects so mind-numbingly boring, anachronistic, and quotidian, I truly felt like they were fucking with me. Polyester brown pants with a matching brown shirt hung proudly in one case. Another case held a few cans of food, and another housed electronics so old, I honestly had to ask what some were (one answer, "to make light shine on wall," did little to clarify).

I kept having the same thought I'd had so many times before during my visit: Is this really the best they can do? If a stuffed animal behind glass is NoKo putting its best foot forward to impress foreigners, then they really need to rethink their strategy. Understand, too, that in this same hall of manufacturing masterpieces, there is no running water in the bathroom.

But the *pièce de résistance* for me was the planetarium, which I believe is inside the technology building. We took a disproportionately long ride in a 300-year-old elevator to the second floor, where the doors opened on complete darkness. Everyone pretended not to notice as the elevator operator escorted us into the abyss. My handlers, the local handlers, the elevator operator, and I stood waiting in the dark for anything to happen. I joked that maybe the Dear Great Leader needed to come give some of the on-the-spot guidance he's so famous for to get the lights to come on. Predictably, no one laughed at my joke but me.

A light came on, and we walked over to the first exhibit, a pendulum.

I think it's crucial to take a moment here to again highlight the fact that we were in a building on a campus dedicated to showcasing Korea's achievements in technology, science, and engineering, built for the express purpose of impressing foreigners and convincing the Korean people their Great Leader is a genius.

As we stood around what looked like a card table with a large sheet of peeling white paper laid over the top and a motionless, weighted wire cable hanging above, the local guide earnestly explained, "This shows the world goes 'round."

"It's a pendulum," I sheepishly offered, not wanting to steal her thunder.

Then she added, "You can see it's divided into twenty-four sections." I couldn't, but this seemed beside the point. "Do you know why?" So while I of course know the answer, I'm starting to doubt myself, because between the cans of food, the absence of lights, and the barely function-ing elevator, this shit is just all so unreal that maybe here in NoKo, the Earth *doesn't* rotate around the Sun.

"Because it takes twenty-four hours for the Earth to rotate around the Sun?" I offered. Correct! Score one for America.

"Look where the pointer is now," she continued. "When we finish our visit, the pointer will have moved one section," she explained. Feeling confident after my last correct response, I countered, "or because the Earth is rotating." Fresh Handler giggled, earning a spot on my "Shit I Think Might Be Real" list.

The local guide then walked me through an interminable series of rudi-mentary graphics akin to what one might find in a high-school astronomy classroom circa 1970, with blurry photographs explaining North Korea's space program, model rockets (which they mistakenly—or not—kept calling missiles), and a detailed account of every satellite they've ever launched. I felt like I should be taking notes but figured the CIA or NSA was probably on it. Nevertheless I started listening for contradictions and inconsistencies and committed to memory what salient facts I could, mainly out of boredom.

Last, my handlers and I were invited to sit for an astronomy presentation, which turned out to be a bunch of white spots on the ceiling that I could not discern one from another, even with the help of a red laser that they seemed to point arbitrarily at things that were not actually illuminated. I wondered whether they were doing this on purpose to make me feel stupid, or if they were just really bad at pointing.

The high-pitched, rousing, urgent, warbling commentary heard everywhere in NoKo, including outside, carried on and on, mispronouncing word after word as it described the universe in terms so basic I couldn't understand a word of it.

I was bored to tears and on the verge of falling asleep when I heard/felt/saw Fresh Handler and Older Handler stand up and walk away. This was highly unusual—one, because my handlers never left me alone anywhere, and two, because I couldn't sort out how they managed to stand up and walk away in a room so dark I couldn't even see my own hands.

After eight days alone in NoKo with no one to *really* talk to but myself, I became momentarily paranoid at being left alone in pitch blackness. There must be a reason, I kept telling myself. What reason I couldn't say to me, but I spent the next few minutes alternating between thoughts of being stuck in North Korea for the rest of my life, and the sad realization that I may have indeed finally lost the plot.

I quelled my fear by mentally devising an "Escape from the Planetarium" plan, using my cell phone as a flashlight, and told myself that if the lights didn't come back on and my handlers weren't back in five minutes....

And just like that the voice stopped, and the one not-burned-out light in the planetarium came back on. I can't remember if my handlers were sitting next to me or not. I was just happy I wasn't going to have to Muay Thai my way out of there using my phone.

As we walked back to the elevator, the local guide paused at the pendulum to say, "See, the pointer moved."

WHO IN THE WORLD AM I? AH, THAT'S THE GREAT PUZZLE!

LEWIS CARROLL

Alice's Adventures in Wonderland

CHAPTER NINETEEN

CLAM BAKE AND A HOT SPA

All week long I had been promised a trip to Nampo for a "clam bake" and a "hot spa," but like everything else in North Korea, reality was but a sliver of itself.

The clam bake turned out to be Driver putting a bunch of clams on a round, metal plate resembling the Con Ed ones you're supposed to avoid stepping on in New York City, because they've been known to electrocute horses and unsuspecting tourists. He then soaked it in gasoline and lit it on fire as my handlers and I watched, sitting on one-foot-by-one-foot stools stationed a foot off the ground, in a parking lot crawling with giant ants that I was very afraid of.

Older Handler would not stop chiding me as Driver was cooking: "Take a photo!" "This is very special!" "All tourists take a photo!" "Here give me camera, I take a photo!" "Why don't you want a photo?" Because…I did not want a photo of a bunch of clams on fire in a parking lot.

And clearly, I had become grumpy, bordering on truculent.

I reminded myself to zip it as she incessantly bossed me around. The sooner it was over, I told myself, the sooner I could go back to my cell and take a hot spa!

And yes, the hot spa turned out to be a lukewarm bath, in a grungy bathtub with nonworking jets, in a dingy bathroom with awful fluorescent lighting—hardly the panacea I had so naively allowed myself to believe in.

Normally a minor setback like this would not induce tears (even while being chedah—North Korean for "let's get drunk!"—and listening to melancholy music). I am generally an exceptionally resilient, adaptable, and low-maintenance traveler, and this bathroom was a lavish palace compared to many I've used throughout the world. But a hot spa it was not. And it was my seventh night traveling solo in NoKo.

I'd been with no one except my handlers and driver—plus local guides who joined us every place I visited—who all proptalked at me for seven straight days and nights at all times (unless I ate alone, or was in my hotel room) with the singular goal of convincing me North Korea is great, and that the Party's and Dear Great Leaders' dogma is spot on. I hadn't so much gone to North Korea as a tourist as I had inadvertently stumbled into a Cult of Kim indoctrination, and they were determined to convert me.

Between their overzealous and overbearing solicitousness and their constant verbal harassment, I felt like I was part tabloid celebrity, part child with super special needs, part prisoner living in some dystopian future—surrounded at all times by people trying to control me. With no chance for any real discourse, it was suffocating and exhausting to be ceaselessly cogitating over my conflicting emotions and thoughts, while navigating the confusing and delicate relationship I had with my handlers—all while trying not to be arrested for an inane infraction such as folding an image of the Dear Great One in half.

There were moments when Fresh Handler would subtly express doubt or disillusionment over life in North Korea, but it was only on my last day that Older Handler finally owned up to the possibility that all may not be paradise in NoKo. She asked me if I wanted to tell her anything. I looked her in the eyes and said earnestly that I could not possibly be the first tourist to tell her that some of the shit they do and say was just pure lunacy…right?

She paused and replied, "To be honest, yes, on the last day sometimes some tourists say such things."

North Korea is really a metaphor for LIFE'S BIG QUESTIONS. What the fuck is going on in this country is just a hop, skip, and jump away from asking: what does it all mean anyway? What do bad and good even mean? And by whose definition? Why do people behave this way? Why is mankind so flawed? Maybe we have everything backwards. Who's to say North Koreans aren't happy? And why is North Korea the worst place on Earth, when there are plenty of other places on Earth giving NoKo a run for its money?

Our clam bake is followed by the hot spa. Only it's not. Older Handler has confused the schedule because our hotel runs the water (as in, *all water*) only from 9:00 p.m. to 10:00 p.m., not 7:00 p.m. to 8:00 p.m. Silly Older Handler.

So instead I am escorted to our hot spa's hotel restaurant for dinner. What this fakarant in Nampo lacks in charm, it makes up for in bad taste. It is, as are all public buildings in NoKo, overly air conditioned, underlit, butt ugly, and fucking loud. I thought the gas clams were dinner, so I had loaded up on those and already feel full. I'm tired, I'm sad, and I want to go home, or at least back to my room.

My handlers and Driver have just started eating, so they allow me to walk back to my room alone. I am temporarily elated. But after seven days of me, myself, and I overanalyzing the shit out of everything in an environment that is a combination of *The Truman Show*, Nazi-occupied Germany, any sitcom from the 1950s minus the fun and funny, and what I can only imagine would be the amalgamation of solitary confinement, regular prison, and a psych ward, culminating in a lukewarm, dingy bath...I felt so inundated by observations, thoughts, feelings of amusement, sadness, confusion, and gratitude that I start to cry (not the noisy kind, just teary).

But I don't indulge in my sobfest for long. Within five minutes of settling into the bath, my phone rings. Startled, I stop crying but do not answer. It stops; I resume crying. The phone rings again. I transition to cry-laughing. I've been away from my handlers for sixteen minutes. I do not answer. The phone rings again, for the third time. Now I'm laugh-crying at the meta, meta, meta-ness of it all.

I know it's over when I hear knocking on my door. It's more than a simple battle of wills; Older Handler will not stop until we've spoken. And while I have the will to persevere, I simply don't care any longer. And besides, I had more cry-laugh-thinking to get back to. And the tub wasn't getting any warmer.

But before accepting defeat and rousing myself from the tub to answer the door, I took this self-portrait to capture the moment.

For me, life is all about moments, and this particular one—laugh-cry-laughing in a hot-not spa somewhere in North Korea while being stalked by my handler, after eating gasoline clams in a parking lot—was too outstanding a moment not to document. It was a great fucking moment—feeling that frustrated, done, and amused at the same time. I wanted to remember always the simultaneous emotions I was experiencing: gratitude for being able to experience what I had, mixed with guilt knowing I'd leave and "betray" my handlers by talking about my experiences the way I have…although I find it very hard to believe that they believed for one second I was buying anything they were selling.

Naked, literally and metaphorically…this moment went on my "Shit I Think Might Be Real" list.

In the morning Older Handler took great pride in emphatically telling me no one had ever remained in the hot spa (gig's up—it's a tub) for more than ten minutes, due to its awesome hotness. "Foreigners" she told me, had "cried out" that the hot spa is so hot, they'd remained in for only eight minutes!

Seeking affirmation, she cheerfully asked how long I'd stayed in. "Thirty minutes," I shot back without missing a beat. I couldn't help myself. It was day eight. Game, back on.

BUT HOW CAN YOU TALK WITH A PERSON IF
THEY ALWAYS SAY THE SAME THING?

LEWIS CARROLL

Through the Looking-Glass

CHAPTER TWENTY

FRIENDS FOR LIFE

'm walking slowly down a long, bare hallway surrounded by my handlers and the local guide as we pass door after locked, closed door. Walking in lock-step a few feet in front of us and behind us are six or seven more local guides, each of whom is wearing—as all local guides everywhere do—a different, vibrantly colored *Chosŏn-ot*, the traditional Korean dress (and the most colorful things in NoKo), with more or less matching hair styles. The full-length, A-line dresses are so poufy that the guides look like they're hovering just above the floor. No one is speaking, so there's utter silence except for the slight sound the dresses make with each seemingly regimented step. I am beyond freezing, so I bundle my arms around myself.

As I hold myself tightly, surrounded on all sides by matching Stepford wives who leave me no chance of escape, I allow myself to imagine that I'm in a straightjacket, being led through the bowels of an insane asylum against my will. It's not such a stretch.

In reality I'm in the International Friendship Exhibition House in Mount Myohyang, a few hours' drive north from Pyongyang. The antithesis of its name, the International Friendship House is basically a giant, tightly secured vault built into the side of a mountain. It holds every single gift ever given to the Kims: a bizarre, insane pantheon to the Dear Great dead Leaders, with a small nod to the new fat one.

The House, like so many other places I'd visited in NoKo, was built with the express purpose of impressing foreigners and convincing the locals that everyone in the whole wide world thinks their Dear Leaders are great. Of course the local handler told me that their Dear Great dead One had the complex built because he loves his people so much he wanted them to have all the gifts instead of keeping the gifts for himself. Whatever its origins, the massive two-building complex totals 100,000 square meters in area and contains more than 200,000 items in 160 rooms.

The buildings sit among verdant, lush, undulating mountains filled with moody, low-hanging clouds and picturesque streams. I want to take photos but am told it's forbidden. "To take photos of nature?" I ask sardonically and then add as I make a sweeping gesture, "I would think your Dear Great One would be all over this." (Obviously it's time for me to go home.)

Older Handler nicely tells me not to worry. She knows I love taking photos and has at times been accommodating, and she assures me that when we are inside later there will be a designated nature photo-taking spot.

We are greeted at the car by our local handler, another beauty with a serene and kind visage. She is particularly adept at the near-silent, urgent whisper voice all the local guides employ. I imagine only the best of the best of the best are chosen for this most prestigious local-guide gig.

When we reach the vestibule of the first building, Local Handler playfully challenges me—Older Handler translates—to try opening the front door, which is flanked by two unsmiling, emotionless, elaborately dressed guards holding automatic rifles. I try the door, but it's like trying to move a container ship with my bare hands. The four-ton metal door does absolutely nothing. Everyone, save for the guards, has a good laugh.

When the doors roll open as if by magic, I'm invited inside, where I'm immediately asked to don fancier-than-normal dirt-prevention shoe covers before being directed to a desk where I'm told to surrender all of my possessions. When I refuse to hand over my wallet—no frickin' way—Local Handler warmly acquiesces. And even after I try to sneak my cell phone past the guards and through the metal detectors and baggage scanner by shoving it into my wallet, Local Handler doesn't lose her cool. The tone of her voice connotes, "I understand your concern, but please don't worry. Your belongings will be safe, I promise." Older Handler reluctantly translates once again, not quite as magnanimously, that perhaps I should try leaving my things behind with the woman at the front desk. I acquiesce.

The next two hours will constitute some of my best travel experiences in NoKo yet.

Each building, or "exhibition" as they are called, is a labyrinth of rooms and long identical hallways punctuated by NoKo's typically over-wrought, grand marble foyers, only these are slightly more palatial. (*Note*: still no running water or toilet paper in the bathroom.) Each room we visit holds glass case after glass case of gifts as perfectly bizarre as North Korea itself.

Rooms are organized by country or region, depending on how many gifts have been proffered by each. They also seem to be categorized by which leader received what gift—like they haven't completely made up their minds which classification system works best. Many, maybe most, of the gifts are from China, "The Soviet Union/USSR," and rogue countries of one type or another, but almost every country is represented—which the

Koreans would be crushed to learn is a function of diplomatic protocol, not Great Leader love.

The American Imperialists, I was happy (?), relieved (?), surprised (?) to see, had contributed a few gifts as well, lest I feel like the one ill-mannered guest to arrive at the party empty-handed. We had a modest but not bad showing: among other odd choices, a couple of Remington bronzes, a crystal ashtray, and a fancy pen (from whom I can't remember), some random branded stuff from CNN, a basketball signed by Michael Jordan that Madeleine Albright bestowed upon the Great One, some more recent additions from the Globetrotters and Dennis Rodman, and a globe surrounded by doves that Billy Graham gave a Great Dear dead One, which both Local Handler and Older Handler were particularly excited about.

I try explaining who Billy Graham was, since they have no idea when I ask, and that given his love of all things religious (including Jesus, whom they are told to disdain) and his distaste for communism (the theory of which they are told is great), I'm surprised they are so zealous about his gift in particular. Fresh Handler and Local Handler listen eagerly; I pause, waiting for Older Handler to translate.

But what is by now a well-established pattern, Older Handler is either unable or unwilling, maybe both, to translate, so my thoughtful, balanced, and well-constructed sermon sounds like she has simply said, "yes."

I'm reminded of one of my favorite scenes in the brilliant film *Lost in Translation*, when Bill Murray's character, Bob, is on set filming a commercial for Suntory Time whiskey, and the hipster director ebulliently instructs him in Japanese about his expectations. When the director stops talking after several minutes, Bob's reticent translator turns to him and says only, "Right side. And, uh, with intensity," to which Bob dubiously replies, "Is that everything? It seemed like he said quite a bit more than that."

Undeterred, I carry on a few minutes longer about how while Billy Graham may have done some good things, his views on women, and Jews, and other religions are a bit off, and how being a TV preacher has a negative connotation, and therefore he is somewhat controversial (not to mention since I don't subscribe to his beliefs, I am personally not the least bit impressed by him). But Older Handler is officially done with translating my dressing down of Saint Billy and his gift of Great Leader love, so she insists we move along.

When Older Handler proudly points to the "largest ivory elephant tusk on Earth," given to the Dear Great Leader by a country unconcerned with poaching, I launch into a diatribe about how grisly, evil, and unconscionable the practice of slaughtering elephants for their tusks is, and how resoundingly reviled a practice it's considered all around the world. Older Handler rewards my unwelcome two cents with her most intense and longest stink eye ever. I stare back, challenging her *not* to translate. Local Handler's interest is beyond piqued. She looks at me, then at Fresh Handler, who is wisely staying clear, and finally at Older Handler. Older Handler finally speaks and probably tells her I need to pee. We move along to the next room of treasures.

There is something ironic about going toe to toe with Older Handler in a place named the International Friendship Exhibition House—and winning—that I find immensely enjoyable and satisfying. It's not because I'm putting her in her place, or any such childish or pedestrian retribution. It's because for the first time since arriving in North Korea, *I actually*

know I'm right. I've been to many countries and have free rein to peruse all the world's history and news. And unlike Older Handler, I know who the gift givers are. Whereas when I mentioned Michael Jackson to Older Handler the day before, she'd responded by asking, "Isn't he the black man who tried to make himself white?" when she points to a terra-cotta Tree of Life statue and tells me what it's not, or when she points out a gift from the Harlem Globetrotters and tells me "they are the best team in America," the conversation is over.

I'm also riveted by the gifts themselves. It's like I'm time traveling through a massive flea market. I try to decipher the meaning behind the hundreds of gifts I see—for example, why the Sandinistas of Nicaragua would have given the Great Dear dead One an upright, stuffed crocodile with a grin on its face that's straddling an ashtray while presenting a tray full of wooden cups—but I can't.

And I've become obsessed with Local Handler, who I would swear keeps giving me the universal look hostages and other people who need rescuing have—the one when their face says nothing's wrong, but their eyes say, "Can you please help get me out of here?" I giggle to myself as I try to decide which of the three Charlie's Angels I, Local Handler, and Fresh Handler would play if this were a movie and not North Korea and I was actually there to bust them both free. Me: Drew Barrymore. Fresh Handler: Lucy Liu. Local Handler: Cameron Diaz. I have no doubt.

We ride a small elevator to the top floor, and I'm guided through a large, empty, dark gift shop and onto a viewing terrace for my previously promised designated nature view and photo opportunity. Although the vista is extraordinary, truly lovely, it does not go unnoticed that by having very carefully art directed the view (the platform allows you to see only a single narrow angle), they've somehow managed to control how you

see Mother Nature inside NoKo, too.

The approved-for-photographing, scenic overview of nature they've unnecessarily reverse engineered into picture-perfect perfection is a metaphor for all that's been wrong with this trip.

I love exploring the world. It's my absolute greatest passion, and I've been traveling my entire life. I made my first international solo trip to Mexico when I was twelve years old. Who I am as a person is fundamentally and inextricably linked to the people I've met and what I've seen and experienced as I've crisscrossed the world. I am a better version of myself when I travel, and each place I visit helps me improve. Travel fosters gratitude, appreciation, independence, curiosity, creativity, knowledge, wisdom, confidence, empathy, joy, and love. It kills fear, ignorance, assumptions, prejudice, preconceived ideas and beliefs, taking things for granted, and uncompromising morals.

Travel makes the world smaller. It's easy to find differences among us. Politics and religion may force us to separate, and the specific routines of daily life may be so different they're unrecognizable; but as sentient beings, we're the same. And the more you travel, the more you viscerally understand just how similar we all are. Even those we find so easy to demonize have their hearts broken. Because travel humanizes those who surround us, "the Chinese," "Russia today said...," and "Japan suffered another..." are no longer dehumanized banter on the news; they are places you've spent time in, people you've met and now care about.

When I travel, I am a cultural ambassador for my country, and for women, and for single women, and for Jewish people—and I never forget this. I remain aware that I am the closest many people I meet will ever come to interacting with another country. I am the first white person, the first Jew, the first American many people have ever seen. I travel with an open heart, and an open mind, with the intention of learning and sharing, and then sharing what I've learned with people back home.

Travel is truly a love affair. But, just like love, it's a two-way street.

And North Korea deprives you of all this. They want you to fall in love with the singular vision of the country they're willing to show you and nothing more.

Everything you do and see is staged and managed. Everyone with whom you are allowed to speak knows what he or she can and cannot say. When there are real people doing ordinary things, you're not allowed to engage. When there are sights deemed too unsightly, the guides pretend they aren't there. When questions are asked that they don't want to answer, or criticisms levied they don't want to hear, they are masterful at staying on point and controlling the message, whether through distraction, redirection, preemptive strike, or when all else fails, just plain old ignoring. There's no sharing, empathizing, or finding common ground; there's only the propaganda tour.

Older Handler was no more interested in what I had to say about the complexities of American politics, and why some people like our president while others may not, than she was in sharing if it was hard to be away from her daughter during the weeks she spent with tourists like me.

Whether I was asking how people in her country are assigned jobs or apartments, or who exactly was allowed to join the Young Pioneers, or why all the hair salons in Pyongyang look exactly the same, or how in the world they managed to keep all 200,000 (or however many—couldn't get a straight answer to this either) gifts in the International Friendship Exhibition House dust free, if it wasn't on the propaganda tour, it wasn't getting answered. You're on a permanent first date with North Korea. And with no chance for any real intimacy, there's no chance for love.

So as I stand there taking photos of their perfect version of nature from their designated nature photo-taking spot—with Older Handler to my left, and Local Handler and Fresh Handler to my right—I decide at long last to just stop trying. My dogged determination to find answers to unanswerable questions and bond where no bonds were allowed to be forged was slowly making me crazy. It's no wonder that when I'd allowed my mind to wander down that hallway, it led me straight to the psych ward.

Back inside and through more hallways, we arrived in a foyer with large wooden doors on either end. Something was about to be revealed that should have struck me as astonishingly weird but no longer was. When we arrived in the foyer, the local large-wood-door-opening guides were sitting when I guess they should have been standing, because they both shot up and apologized to Local Handler as if we'd caught them two (or three) sheets to the wind, playing strip poker.

I honestly can't remember who exactly was explaining what—it was an amorphous mix of urgent, excited, and very hushed whispering describing what I was about to see. Inside the first room would be a life-size image of the first dead Great One that one or many of them told me (warned me?) was so lifelike that "many people say" it's like you're standing in the presence of the Dear Great dead One himself, only he's not dead at all (they, of course, said this in a far more cogent, reverent, obsequious, effusive, and fulsome way). I guess to ensure I understood the gravity of the situation, one of the eight handlers positioned in the foyer added, "many people have fainted" and "even cried out!" upon seeing the Great Wax One, so I should prepare myself.

I bit my tongue hard, determined to stick to my recently implemented five-minutes-ago new plan of "no questions asked/no talking back," and therefore let pass the 300,000 questions and comments I had swirling around in my head.

I was ushered to the opposite end of the room. We walked in a perfectly straight line, shoulder to shoulder, as silently and solemnly as one would if one were walking to one's own beheading. When we reached the Great Wax One, we bowed deeply and for a very long time. So long I nearly started laughing because I couldn't figure whether I was waiting for *them* to stop bowing or they were waiting for *me*. I figured you don't get anywhere in life without taking a shot, so I stood up, and they followed.

This was the point at which I thought, well, North Korea has outdone itself. I'm in batshit-crazy town. And the Great Wax One actually did look pretty real, standing there amid fake nature.

We stared at him for a while, until an appropriate amount of time had passed and I was told to move along. Which begged the question: what constitutes an appropriate amount of time to stare at a life-size wax statue of a Dear dead Great Leader whom everyone thinks is still running the country, while standing in an underground bunker in middle-of-nowhere North Korea surrounded by matching handlers? Answer: approximately two very long minutes.

The room on the other end was similarly surreal and creepy, and we followed the same drill. If I remember correctly, it was first Great dead One and his wife and second dead One as a baby riding a horse, or something like that. As you might imagine, all the propaganda starts to blend and become one after a week or so.

By that point I was ready to pack up and leave, and hoped this was the grand finale. But nope; we still had the other building to see. As we walked across the driveway from one building to the next, a squadron of uniformed guards performing some type of drill marched past us. Having eclipsed us by a minute or so, they reached the second building first and were in the middle of an elaborate changing-of-the-guards ceremony when we reached the front door of building number two.

I failed to catch myself before innocently commenting that many countries share the same custom at important landmarks, like Buckingham Palace in London. "Totally different," snapped Older Handler. And…I'm off yet again. My period of self-imposed "just shut the fuck up already" lasted roughly ten minutes. "Well, why do you say that? It's the same concept, isn't it? Have you seen the changing of the guards at Buckingham Palace? You know they do the same thing at the Gyeong-bokgung Palace in Seoul, South Korea, too" (now I'm really playing with fire…do not pass go, go directly to jail).

As we stepped inside I asked Older Handler to ask Local Handler how often they change guards. "She doesn't know," Older Handler replied without asking Local Handler.

"How can she not know? She works here, doesn't she?"

"Not her department. She works inside."

I've completely fallen off the wagon, "Well, can you at least please ask her for me?"

Korean, Korean, Korean, "She doesn't know."

I looked at the former love of my life for the last hour and give her the stink eye while saying to I guess anyone, or myself, "She doesn't know. And yet she works here. And walks outside. Why is this secret information? What do you think I can possibly do with this information? In other countries this is actually published information because they are proud of their changing-of-the-guard ceremonies—it's something tourists specifically turn up to see."

Not only am I getting nowhere fast and annoying everyone, risking deportation or worse, but also I've been unkind to poor Local Handler, who has done nothing wrong. Quite the opposite, she's been positively lovely throughout. And over what? I want to cry. And just like that, for the first and last time in North Korea, I moved myself along.

Seems I'm the best of myself everywhere in the world except North Korea, and in line at the Starbucks at Fourteenth and Sixth in Manhattan.

Our tour of the second building (which looked exactly like the first) completed, Local Handler walked Fresh Handler, Older Handler, and me back to our car. I still felt badly about my (mental) row with Local Handler, and I wanted to make amends. I wanted her to know how much I appreciated her time that day and all the kindness and patience she'd shown me. I wanted to somehow acknowledge whatever I thought I had seen in her eyes that made me feel like we had managed to connect.

Once Older Handler and Fresh Handler were halfway into the car, I quickly turned back away from the car toward Local Handler and tapped her on the arm. I took both her hands in mine and looked her in the eyes and said in English, "I want to thank you; you've been so kind. I'm so glad I met you, and I wish you all the best." She gave my hand a slight squeeze, smiled, and said in English back to me, "Thank you." A little bit like we were real new friends.

I DIDN'T MEAN IT! PLEADED POOR ALICE.

LEWIS CARROLL

Alice's Adventures in Wonderland

CHAPTER TWENTY-ONE

DRIVER

Driver was like an avuncular yakuza with bad manners. But for some reason I liked him from the moment we were introduced in the airport parking lot. He spoke no English. Or he was fluent and faking it. But what would be the point?

He was either in his late sixties or early forties. I honestly cannot remember which. I do, however, remember being really surprised by how old or how young he looked when Older Handler told me his age. His visage had a sort of timeless oldness to it. Like alcoholics who live where there's nothing but sun.

He had a gold tooth or two, spiky hair, and a generally gruff exterior. He was slight and not particularly tall, but he had the air of somebody who could and would viciously tear any enemy apart, regardless of whether or not it was deserved. I always felt bad for having these feelings about him, because he was probably a decent man. I was judging a book by its cover, a man by his looks.

Except he did violently stomp to death an innocent bug that I had pains-takingly rescued from our car just mere seconds ago…while he watched.

Though I am pathologically afraid of insects, I refuse to kill anything unless all other options are exhausted and circumstances demand it. So instead of squashing or swatting said insects to death, I force myself to mollycoddle the things I fear most and try to gingerly expel them (lest I accidentally kill one) from wherever I am.

Driver had watched me carefully eject the bug from our car with the obvious intention of keeping the bug alive. And it had been just the day before when I'd had a whole conversation with Driver and Older Handler—who I doubted by that point was accurately translating anything to anyone on my behalf—at the DMZ (when I was asking them to pull our car over to shoo the scary flying insect out) about me not killing things, and being a vegetarian, and thinking all beings' lives have equal value. And that's probably where I lost Older Handler's desire for accuracy.

Not to mention, if I managed to get the bug out of the car, did he not think I would also be capable of stomping on it myself? Clearly stomping to death a hapless insect already down for the count is far easier than ensuring its safe passage out of an automobile.

The ironic thing is that Driver meant to be valiant. He'd killed the bug *for* me, not to spite me. Recall how I'd literally squealed from fear at DMZ, not because of the danger of the place but because of a fly. And I'd made no bones about it…insects are *persona non grata* number one.

Because he knew this, Driver brutally stomped the bug—I am not embellishing—it was a Falklands War disproportionate-style stomp. In response to which I involuntarily slap-smacked him on the arm. It was a knee-jerk reaction. We slap-smack each other as punctuation marks all the time at home! C'mon! (For example, I would have just slap-smacked you there.)

As soon as I smack him, I realize what I've done. But it's too late. I can see in his eyes that I've hurt his feelings and somehow made him feel stupid or rejected. In one fell swoop I seem to have destroyed so much. Our tenuous relationship, so hard-won, has now been jeopardized. I feel truly awful. Especially since—next to Waiter with accent *horrible*, and Fresh Handler—I love Driver third best.

I immediately start apologizing in English, while alternately begging Older Handler to apologize for me in Korean (she's an unreliable bitch, but she's all I got) and explain to Driver that we slap-smack each other all the time at home as a gesture of endearment, blah blah, and on and on. I blab so fast that I fumble over my own words of contrition, and Older Handler stops translating altogether. No doubt in an effort to ameliorate hurt feelings, Older Handler instead knowingly turns to me and states the obvious, "You hurt Driver's feelings."

It takes only microseconds for Driver's hurt to turn to humiliation crossed with embarrassment, like the feeling you have when you tell a joke that doesn't land. Then he transitions to mad. His face now inscrutable, he turns his back to me and walks into the fakarant.

Lunch rolls like a step-family dinner—that is, awkwardly. Driver isn't making eye contact. Now I feel mad-bad and wish I could say something like, "I'm sorry that you killed an innocent bug, causing me to accidentally punch you on the arm, and now you won't even look at me, let alone speak to me via Older Handler, even though I've apologized a billion times, and I feel *gutted* about this. Please don't be mad." I'm also *really happy* he's so unabashedly hurt; that means he's experiencing actual feelings, and there's nothing the Party can do about it. Try as it might to present its citizens as perfect beings, Koreans are human, too.

Driver was an enigma: sometimes chivalrous and gallant, sometimes just plain trashy.

At the clam bake he pretended the cone-topped, plastic squeeze bottle was his penis, and that the oil spraying from it to kindle the gasoline flames into the fiery inferno needed to char our clams was his pee. He was chedah (we all were), so we were laughing as he "peed" in giant circles and figure eights with that ever-present cigarette dangling from his mouth. But even as we laughed, there was a sense of menace that so pervaded his demeanor it was hard to shake. As usual, I felt truly awful about judging him so harshly. He was probably just an aging bad boy, with misleadingly ugly shoes.

I always tried my best to correctly say "thank you" in Korean whenever he let me in or out of our car. *Gamsahamnida.* I got it right once. If you're sounding it out loud right now and thinking to yourself, she must be an idiot, because that's easy to say, try it without this book in front of you.

I didn't have a cheat sheet. And even though I'd learned 169 new English words using Kaplan's vocab app on my phone, I couldn't get this single Korean word right.

Because we visited at least eight places each day—and he picked me up from and dropped me off at my hotel each day *and* let me in and out of the car for lunch, dinner, and bathroom stops—I estimate that I probably thanked him the wrong way twenty-two times per day. That had to annoy the shit out of him. But every time I pronounced *gamsaham-nida* wrong—which, by the way, I managed to say the wrong way exactly the same way every time but could not manage the right way twice—he'd smile or laugh with me at my "oops!" Like he actually enjoyed my gaffes. He came off like a pro linebacker who shows up at the dog park with a Chihuahua instead of a pit bull.

I'd brought sunglasses with me as gifts for my NoKo team. You're advised to bring gifts to give halfway through your trip, in addition to monetary tips at the end of your stay. Not knowing how many handlers I'd have or if they'd be male or female, I'd brought three different unisex styles and a fourth more feminine pair. I presented the sunglasses at lunch one day, inviting Older Handler, Fresh Handler, and Driver to each select the style that suited their taste best. Driver practically knocked Fresh Handler over lunging for the girlie one.

He was a tough guy in a cat eye. He wore the frames with pride.

Driver smoked at every opportunity, and he smelled rank as a result. Eventually I had to ask Older Handler to ask Driver not to smoke just before getting back in the car, that's how bad he smelled. But he took the news like a gentleman and a champ. He immediately stopped smoking anywhere near me or our car. And soon his smoking became fodder for familial-like banter between the two of us—me teasing him about how his disgusting smoking habit was going to kill him, and him hurling back insults at meals about how weird I was for not eating meat. Our "Shit I Think Might Be Real" list teasing made me feel like we were becoming friends, or so I thought, and best of all required no Older Handler translating.

Sometimes when Driver and I were joking around and having fun, I would feel real affection for him, so I would tell him I was going to miss him, and he would tell me the same. And I meant it. And I do. Not the way you miss a best friend or your family or anything close. But there was something there. And I think he felt it too.

NEITHER OF THE OTHERS TOOK THE LEAST
NOTICE OF HER GOING, THOUGH SHE LOOKED
BACK ONCE OR TWICE, HALF HOPING THAT
THEY WOULD CALL AFTER HER: THE LAST

TIME SHE SAW THEM, THEY WERE TRYING TO
PUT THE DORMOUSE INTO THE TEAPOT.

LEWIS CARROLL   *Alice's Adventures in Wonderland*

CHAPTER TWENTY-TWO

THE GYNECOLOGIST

I am waiting alone in front of the made-to-order omelet station at the breakfast buffet in the Koryo Hotel. The station is a small, free-standing, electric frying pan/skillet thing that had to be thirty years old and resembled the brownish-colored aluminum one with the Teflon cooking surface that I used to illegally use in my college dorm room in the 1980s. Here the chef cooked only fried eggs that he somehow managed to serve cold, congealed, and covered in oil, even when freshly made.

Because I am lost in thought, pondering the unique cooking skills required to heat eggs enough to transmute them from raw to cooked while still keeping them cold, I fail to immediately notice the man standing by my side.

When I look up and over at him, I'm beyond surprised to see he's young, cute, and not Chinese (unlike the overwhelming majority of tourists I've encountered).

"Hi," he says. He's obviously new in town, so not afraid to talk to strangers yet.

"Hi," I whisper back.

We quickly exchange names, ranks, and serial numbers in a tone slightly above hushed, and I return to my assigned seat.

As I sit buttering my eggs with strawberry jelly (it was the only way to get them down), he walks over and asks if he's allowed to sit with me instead of at his assigned table. We both look around the room, conducting a synchronized threat assessment of what might happen to us if we break the rules. Not much, we conclude, so down he sits.

We don't have much time—we both have to meet our handlers downstairs in the lobby in eight minutes, at 8:00 a.m. on the dot—so we debrief each other quickly.

He's a twenty-six-year-old Irishman who lives somewhere outside Dublin, is a pediatric surgeon, and incredibly, just like me, is traveling alone. He's spent the past six months on holiday with his mates traveling around the world—but unlike him, they've wisely skipped this, his last stop and gone home. He just arrived the day before and will leave NoKo in just over a day on the same flight as I.

I calmly tell him I'm from New York, and feel like I'm about to lose my mind because Older Handler is a nut job, and all anyone's done for the past eight days is lie to me and give me the stink eye, and that I'm dehydrated from not drinking enough water because it makes me have to pee too often, which is a pain in the ass because every time I have to pee they have to find me an approved bathroom, and poor Fresh Handler has to go with me, and that I've eaten nothing but chocolate bars and really bad eggs since I've been there. And then my projectile word vomiting really begins.

I can't control myself. It's like I haven't seen another human being in a year. As it all pours out between bites of strawberry-jelly-covered eggs, his face registers a mix of sympathy and fear. I feel compelled to tell him that I'm not crazy (a claim that always sounds crazy), that I'm a normal person (ditto) with a good job where other people even work *for* me! I'm a homeowner! Not some lunatic who babbles uncontrollably about Older Handler and conspiracy theories to anyone who innocently says hello.

When I take a breath, he explains that his handlers, both young women, are really nice and really cool, and they joke around with him, and he jokes around with them, and they're pretty lax about stuff and remiss with all the rules.

UMMM. Wait a minute! I didn't even know this was a possibility!

And then I get it...they have a schoolgirl crush on Dr. Handsome. No twisted, bitter, envious, autocratic, despotic Older Handler craziness in his camp.

Oh and it also seems that for whatever reason—my guess, wishful thinking—his handlers are convinced he's a gynecologist, not a pediatric surgeon, and thus have been querying him for tips on how they can have twins.

After my visits to the "multiples exhibit" at both the hospital and the orphanage—and after having pummeled Older Handler with questions about why the Dear Great Leader likes twins and triplets until I thought she was going to smack me—I'm feeling pretty much like an expert (it's a conspiracy). I tell him everything I am one hundred percent convinced I definitely do or do not know.

The hands on the giant clock above the buffet tell us we better move it or lose it. Our handlers are expecting us now. My team is driving to Mount Myohyang, and his team is hanging in Pyongyang, so for the moment we say good-bye.

When I see Older Handler in the lobby, I have a giant smile on my face. My eggs may not have been tasty, but breakfast was cathartic.

I tell her I met another tourist traveling alone! Just like me! Who's from Ireland! Whom I told all about how fucking nuts you are for eight straight minutes! (I left that last bit out.) And how now I feel as giddy as his handlers! (Same with that.)

OLDER HANDLER: You mean the gynecologist?

ME: He's a pediatric surgeon. Not a gynecologist.

OLDER HANDLER: He delivers twins.

ME: No, he operates on babies.

OLDER HANDLER, *intractable, silence.*

Late the next afternoon, on our drive from Mount Myohyang back to Pyongyang, Older Handler is apologizing to me. It's my last night in NoKo, so she wants the four of us—Fresh Handler, Driver, her, and me—to have a fun dinner together and make chedah. But tonight's restaurant is Korean BBQ style, so "only meat."

I appreciate her sincerity. She's made a concerted effort throughout my stay to ensure no one feeds me anything with meat in it, which I'm very grateful for (and further convinced that on the rotating schedule of fakarants, it must be this joint's turn). I tell her not to worry, that it's not a problem at all. Quite frankly, I think to myself, I'd literally eat the table-cloth if it ensured I'd be on the next plane out tomorrow.

273

Unconvinced I'll be okay with only rice, she adds, "The gynecologist will be there, too."

ME: He's a pediatric surgeon.

When we arrive at the fakarant, Dr. Irish, his driver, and his two adoring fans are already seated and have started eating and drinking. We sit at the table next to theirs, and Older Handler immediately takes charge:

OLDER HANDLER: We make chedah! You drink wine! We get wine!

Older Handler loves wine.

Wine is what Older Handler affectionately calls *Soju*, which is decidedly not wine but basically pure alcohol. I'm not sure if she actually thinks *Soju* is wine or if she's using the word wine euphemistically to mask her fondness for the hard stuff, but I find her misnomer endearing.

The first time Older Handler offered me wine, I innocently took a generous sip, expecting it to taste more like Chardonnay than rubbing alcohol crossed with fire. Once I stopped coughing and tearing uncontrollably, I decided I liked it, and from then on Older Handler has made sure I've ordered—and paid for—wine whenever it's available.

Several bottles of *Soju* arrive, and for the last time I also buy Driver a few beers (he's a beer guy, not a wine guy). Within minutes we're all sloshed. (Once, after Driver had enjoyed a two-Large Beer lunch, I asked Older Handler about drunk driving in Korea. Her response: "Yes, we have.") We "chedah" each other, and we "chedah" Dr. Irish and his posse, and they "chedah" us back. Sitting there together, everyone drunk, smiling and laughing, it almost seems normal.

I feel overwhelmingly and irrationally sentimental. I can't believe I'm leaving in the morning. I've spent so much time wishing it was over, and now it is. Only now I sort of wish it wasn't, even though I still can't wait to leave. It felt exactly like the one time I went to sleep-away camp, which I also hated and couldn't wait to leave. But the last night, when the entire camp sat around a giant bonfire, singing songs and reminiscing about the summer's events, I cried along with the others, not wanting it to end but desperate for it to be over.

In the two days that have passed since I first met Dr. Irish at breakfast, he's been dragged around on his own propaganda tour. While his handlers have maintained their you're-so-dreamy laissez-faire approach to his care and handling, they've failed to convince him that North Korea is anything other than repressed and insane. As we sit sharing stories and comparing notes under our breath, a giant wave of relief washes over me: for the first time since I arrived in Korea, someone else is confirming the crazy.

When Older Handler and Driver are engaged in conversation, I use the opportunity to pitch Fresh Handler on the idea of escape, having spent an entire week telling her why New York City is so great, why she'd love it so much, and what great friends we could be.

"I wish!" she giggled into her hand so Older Handler couldn't hear or see.

I fucking knew it!

"Me, too," I said solemnly in return.

That I would never be allowed to see or speak to Fresh Handler ever again, in any manner, was a strange and sad reality.

The next morning we're all gathered in the lobby, ready to go.

I exit the Koryo Hotel for one last time. I get into my car with my handlers, and Dr. Irish gets into his car with his, and we both depart for the airport.

As I sit in the back seat one last time, staring out the window at a city I can't wait to leave, quietly contemplating what it all meant, the car carrying Dr. Irish, pediatric surgeon, speeds by us.

"Ah!" Older Handler excitedly peeps, as she points. "Do you know whose car that was?"

"No, whose?" I ask rhetorically.

"The gynecologist's!" she says excitedly.

And for a moment, I really do love Older Handler.

Driver pulls our car into the parking lot of the tiny, old, operating airport (which, NoKo-style, sits maybe a yard from a large, brand-new, closed airport), turns off the car, and gets out. He's been uncharacteristically quiet during the drive there. He fetched my bag from the boot of the car and without looking me in the eyes, put it down by my side. I handed him his tip and motioned for a hug or something to say a proper farewell, but he turned away and got back in the car without saying one word—not thank you; not even good-bye.

And that was that.

Older Handler and Fresh Handler escorted me inside the terminal building. My eyes started welling up with tears. I always tear up in airports—I'm not great at transitions—but also I'm sad-ish at saying goodbye, and Driver's surprising behavior had upset me, leaving me feeling even more discombobulated over how our goodbye was about to go down.

Turned out the same as it had with Driver, only they thanked me for their tips.

Maybe affectionate farewells aren't allowed in North Korea, particularly those involving foreigners? Or maybe their snubs were coping mechanisms—the only way to keep their emotions in check to avoid trouble? Or maybe I'd read everything wrong, and none of them had ever liked me, believing all along I was nothing more than a vile American Imperialist?

I'll never know.

I SHOULDN'T KNOW YOU AGAIN IF WE DID MEET, HUMPTY DUMPTY REPLIED IN A DISCONTENTED TONE, GIVING HER ONE OF HIS FINGERS TO SHAKE; *YOU'RE SO EXACTLY LIKE OTHER PEOPLE.*

LEWIS CARROLL

Through the Looking-Glass

CHAPTER TWENTY-THREE

THEY'RE ONLY HUMAN

We were driving someplace outside of Pyongyang. I don't remember where, but we'd been in the car a while when we came upon a massive, sprawling construction site with half-built, deconstructed apartment buildings stretching for blocks in every direction. There were thousands and thousands of men laboring away in the hot sun using manual tools and dressed in their normal, ragged street clothes or military uniforms. It was shocking to see a construction site of that scale, with men perilously clinging to the sides of the buildings and dangling from windows with no safety gear on, hauling wheelbarrows piled high with construction debris, and doing the work machines usually do. Their movements looked frenzied and chaotic, like panicked ants zigzagging in every direction.

I sat transfixed, staring out the window, trying to understand what I was seeing. Normally Older Handler would have been incessantly talking, forcing me to look at her instead of out the window, her normal tactic to prevent me from seeing anything she didn't want me to see. But she was silent. I glanced at her to see why. She was staring out the window, too.

"It's so awful. They look like slaves," I said softly, still looking at her.

She shifted her gaze back to me, and her eyes said what she could not. Then she sighed and looked away.

North Korean citizens are brainwashed from birth to believe that North Korea is superior to every other country in every single way; that their Great Leaders are omnipotent beings who must be revered; and that America, Japan, and South Korea are their mortal enemies, poised to attack their country at any moment.

To ensure compliance with these beliefs, the North Korean people are systemically and systematically enslaved in thought and action. The Cult of Kim permeates every aspect of their lives. Their schools, jobs, and social activities are all part of the indoctrination process. They are denied all access to outside information of any kind. The only knowledge imparted to them is what the Party wants them to know, all of which is reinforced through social molding. Self-expression, freedom of thought, social discourse to effect change, and personal beliefs of any kind are relegated to private thoughts. They are told how to live, where to live, what to do, what to study, what job to do, if they can drive, if they can travel, where they can go, with whom they can speak. Denied any opportunity to shape their own lives, they are robbed of all autonomy, and live in fear of the Regime and one another knowing that any sign of doubt, dissent, or disagreement is intolerable, and that there is a very steep price to pay should they dare step out of line.

By instilling profound fear, hatred of their enemies and unshakable loyalty and commitment to their Dear Great Leader, the Regime has managed to maintain absolute control.

But for people like Older Handler, Fresh Handler, and Driver—who regularly interact with foreigners like me, who are eager to share information, foster understanding, and build relationships—the realization that so much of what they've been told their entire lives is a lie has to invoke a certain cognitive dissonance. I'd read somewhere that the prisoners on Alcatraz could hear the sounds of San Francisco—music and conversation—emanating from the city, and that these sounds of freedom so close, not their incarceration, were what tortured them most. I spent a lot of time wondering and worrying if my handlers weren't suffering the same fate.

I think Older Handler knew down deep inside that North Korea was absurd and that all the Great Dear Leader stuff was nonsense. But her lifelong indoctrination and absolute entrenchment in North Korean society made it impossible for her to dismiss her beliefs and reject her life.

Or maybe not. Maybe she really did believe everything she told me.

I had these moments with Older Handler when a glimmer of recognition would cross her face, or she would gesture to indicate tacit agreement, or she would say something that sounded sincere, and I would feel a real connection to her, something approximating friendship. Older Handler would cease being "Older Handler, Blind Enforcer of Insane Rules" and instead become "Older Handler, Real Person Capable of Complex Thought." But then the moment would evaporate, as if she'd shaken herself out of a reverie and back into the reality of NoKo, where her job was to make me believe North Korea was the greatest place on Earth, and she couldn't be happier there.

As a result, I was always second-guessing myself with her. I one-hundred-percent believed she didn't believe anything she was saying and was just biding her time, and I also believed I was completely wrong.

We were stopped at a light in the car one afternoon when a group of people passed by us all wearing the same wide-brim hats. When I asked Older Handler why, she said something about how they'd all just returned from their two-week service, working the rice fields. She then explained that every citizen, including her, must work in the rice fields for two weeks each year, and that she had just served her time in the fields a few weeks ago. I was so shocked by her admission that I asked whether it was hard work and sad, being away from her family and job. By reflex she gave me a look that said something along the lines of, "Of course it's hard working the rice fields, you moron," but caught herself almost instantly, smiled and said, "It's my honor."

Or one afternoon at the "book and stamp shop" in Pyongyang (which sold nothing but books written by or about the Great Leaders and other propaganda), Older Handler kept insisting I buy a DVD compilation of rabble-rousing speeches and military parades. I politely declined, but she was relentless. Finally, to put an end to the conversation, I informed her, "No one really uses DVDs in my country anymore. In fact I don't even have a DVD player, and most computers no longer have DVD drives." She ceased speaking, and her face registered a bona fide mix of confusion and disbelief: if North Korea is the greatest and most advanced country in the world, and we use DVDs, then why doesn't America? As I started to explain the concept of on-demand and streaming services, she cut me off, "You buy stamps." Her beatific smile had returned.

It made me wonder yet again if all her bluster and grandiloquence was meant to convince herself that life in North Korea was great, as much as it was meant to convince me.

I suspected Fresh Handler had a better grip on reality than Older Handler did.

I'd seen her giggle at my sarcastic retorts about NoKo too many times to

283

believe otherwise, and from what I'd gleaned from conversation, she'd been exposed to Western culture throughout her life and liked it.

During our visit to the Monument to the Foundation of the Workers' Party, an enormous monument, Fresh Handler and I, as usual, had to use the bathroom. (Much of our bonding time was toilet related.)

The closest bathroom was in a building that also housed some type of art exhibit, which we stopped to visit before walking back to where Older Handler and Driver were waiting for us. As we walked around the gallery of bad art, our conversation turned from paintings to movies. Fresh Handler excitedly offered that she'd seen several American movies when she'd been at university. I told her I was surprised and asked her which ones. The names escape me now, but I remember several starred Hilary Duff or Amanda Bynes. She was so excited and animated describing the movies and so pleased when I told her I'd seen a few of them, too. When I asked her which movie was her favorite, she sheepishly answered that she'd loved them all and thought they were "so funny."

One movie was set in New York City, so our conversation shifted again. I whispered to her how New York City was full of people from all over the world, and how you could hear every language imaginable just walking down the street. I told her how every morning I take a taxi to work and have drivers from far-flung places like Sudan or Pakistan. I told her there were thousands of restaurants and stores within miles of my apartment, and cineplexes capable of showing twenty movies at a time. She soaked it all in like a child listening to a favorite story. Then I told her I thought she would love New York City and that if she ever wanted to visit, or live there, she was welcome to stay with me anytime. She looked at me and wistfully said, "Oh, yes, I really want to!" And I managed to forget for a minute that would never happen.

Fresh Handler's brother, father, and mother had gone to university, too, and were all professionals (doctor, teacher, and doctor, respectively). When I asked her to describe her home to me—if it was nice like the beautiful, modern apartment buildings in Pyongyang that no one seemed to live in, or not so nice, like most of the other buildings—she was honest, telling me she lived in a "so-so nice" building "with two rooms" that her whole family shared. When I posed the same question to Older Handler, she answered something along the lines of, "Yes of course! Very nice!"

One afternoon we were in Manpok Valley for a scheduled walk. Fresh Hander had gone in search of a bathroom so Older Handler and I opted to sit down near a river to wait. During our brief time alone I told Older Handler she could ask me anything she wanted to—whether about me or America or another country, anything, and if I knew the answer I would tell her the absolute honest truth.

Without a moment's hesitation, she asked me to explain the difference between hard currency and soft currency.

"What? That's it?" That's all you want to know? In the whole wide world?" I was incredulous.

She added, "And is the Chinese RMB hard currency?"

Disappointed this was not to be a bonding moment, I took a breath and began explaining hard currency. Then a thought crossed my mind: maybe she was planning her escape. I smiled at Older Handler and continued.

North Korea is a country of secrets, lies, and questions with no answers. It was as much a psychological journey as a tourist experience for me, and I was profoundly affected by my time there.

North Korea is easy to hate and categorize as evil, because it is. And it's particularly easy to make fun of because so many things about it are so fucking ridiculous. But assuming that *North Koreans* are the same as *North Korea* is a mistake. Just like us, they're only human. Separate from the Party, and apart from their Dear Great Leaders, North Koreans are real people.

And I could never stop wondering what kind of people my handlers could or would have been had they been born anywhere else. Or the person I might be had I been born there.

OLDER HANDER (LEFT) AND FRESH HANDLER (RIGHT).

I KNOW WHO I WAS WHEN I GOT UP THIS MORNING, BUT I THINK I MUST HAVE BEEN CHANGED SEVERAL TIMES SINCE THEN.

LEWIS CARROLL

Alice's Adventures in Wonderland

POSTSCRIPT

I departed Pyongyang International Airport the morning of Friday July 4, transiting through Beijing. And through the miracle of flight, even with a significant delay, I still arrived home that same evening, just in time to see New York City's spectacular fireworks display illuminate the skies over Lower Manhattan, the Brooklyn Bridge, and One World Trade Center, right from the comfort of my living room couch.

I cried silent tears of joy and gratitude for having been born into the life I was, and I cried, too, at the irony: I'd had North Korea for breakfast, one of the least free places on Earth, and the Fourth of July, N.Y.C., U.S.A., the apotheosis of freedom, for dinner.

On Sunday while out running errands, I called my local mani-pedi place, Pau Hana, to see if they could squeeze me in. Unlike the thirty other places within walking distance of my house, Pau Hana is tiny, warm, and welcoming and decorated in a Hawaiian theme (I love Hawaii). They don't usually take walk-ins, so I was shocked when they said they could squeeze me in. I rushed right over.

As soon as I sat down and put my feet in the water, the super-nice, adorable nail tech who always takes care of me asked where I'd been the past few weeks. She's from South Korea.

When I told her North Korea, she was shocked but not as shocked as the woman in the chair next to mine. "Did I hear you right," she asked, "that you just returned from North Korea?" When I replied yes, she excitedly pointed to the woman sitting next to her and said, "So did my friend."

"You just got back from North Korea?" I asked incredulously.

"Yes!"

Turns out she'd not only recently returned from North Korea, but in fact works for Koryo Tours, the very company through which I'd booked my independent tour. And even more serendipitously, she works in the exact same, very tucked away, little office in Beijing where, just weeks before, I'd been to pick up my visa.

We'd literally just missed seeing each other by days in both North Korea and Beijing but were now sitting here one seat apart, in this tiny nail salon in Cobble Hill, Brooklyn (which is the smallest neighborhood in Brooklyn, by far, by the way). And I hadn't even had an appointment.

Even crazier, she didn't live in Cobble Hill, or Brooklyn, or even the United States, for that matter. She lives in London and travels back and forth to NoKo but just happened to be getting a pedicure next to me— one of the few Americans to have been to NoKo—only a couple of days after she herself was there, thanks to her company.

I'm well known to have a Ph.D. in knockout coincidences, but this was all pretty great, even by my standards.

She asked me who my handlers were. When I told her Fresh Handler's name, she said, "Never heard of her." But when I gave her the name of Older Handler, I swear, the very first words out of her mouth were, "Oh, she's crazy, and everybody knows it! You poor thing!" And then dropped other words along the lines of *mean, bitter, strict, insane,* and *how in the world did you deal with her for ten straight days,* to help round out her description.

VIN-DI-CA-TION.

I knew there had to be a reason that life with Older Handler was such a pain in my ass.

As I'd suspected all along, she may have had her pride, but she wasn't all that happy. She wanted to be a businesswoman not a guide. She loved her Dear Great Supreme dead Leaders, sure; but she also dug the life she'd been introduced to via people like me. She was no dummy. She'd had a taste and wanted more. And I had been a constant reminder of all she could not have—and everything she'd been told to revile.

She liked me, and she hated me. And I felt the same. Only I kind of really liked her and admired her in a weird way. And actually I hadn't hated her at all; she just annoyed the crap out of me. I still think about Older Handler all the time. She was a complicated character, a Gordian knot of a woman. And I wish I could have known her better.

SHE GENERALLY GAVE HERSELF VERY
GOOD ADVICE, (THOUGH SHE VERY SELDOM
FOLLOWED IT)...

LEWIS CARROLL

Alice's Adventures in Wonderland

SEEING IS NOT BELIEVING

Everything written herein is true, to the best of my memory. I took very few notes while in NoKo for fear that, if they were found, I or my handlers would get in trouble. But the main reason is that I went to North Korea simply as a tourist, with no intention of writing this book.

As I've said, I love exploring the world and sharing what I see. I usually post photos to Instagram and Facebook while I'm traveling, along with thoughts or stories about my photos, funny or interesting things I see or that happen to me. And sometimes when I return home, I'll transfer these stories into my poorly maintained blog.

Of course this was impossible while I was in North Korea. But I knew I'd want to share things the second I got home, so I made a conscious effort to commit to memory the insanely funny, and just plain insane, events and conversations that were happening every day.

On those occasions when something was said or something happened that I knew I would want to recall verbatim, I would throw caution to the wind and write it down as a cryptic note on my iPhone, using a weird shorthand I've developed over a lifetime of scribbling notes as fast as I can (consonants only, incorrect spellings, and word substitutions known only to me, etc.). This, combined with the normal and inevitable iPhone typos and automatic word replacements made me reasonably confident my notes would be illegible. But just to be sure, I split individual notes up across different entries or applications (half in one note, half in another, with misleading headers; half in a note, half as a contact, and so forth). But having grown unreasonably paranoid, I still kept relatively few such notes.

As soon as I cleared immigration in Beijing, I went straight to the airline lounge and started typing out everything I wanted to remember onto my iPhone notes application (an arduous task). The night I arrived home, I immediately appended much greater detail to my list (far more comfortably from my computer keyboard). I still had no intention of writing a book. However, I've learned as I've gotten older that I remember far less than I think I will, and this was one trip I never wanted to forget—and I couldn't wait to begin sharing photos and stories on Facebook.

The morning after I returned home, my photo assistant, Rachel, arrived. Normally I'll tell her myriad stories as we sort through my photos, deciding which to post to Facebook and my website. This time, before saying a word, I turned on my voice recorder and then let it rip, transcribing our hours-long conversation (*read*: soliloquy) while everything was still very fresh in my mind, so I'd remember my trip for the rest of my life, plus have everything correct for Facebook and my blog.

Then about a month later, having read my Facebook posts, James Altucher asked if I would do a podcast on "What's really going on in North Korea" for his show, *The James Altucher Show*. I hadn't stopped obsessing over my trip or talking about my experiences in North Korea since arriving home, so I jumped at the chance. Following the podcast,

I was sent a transcript of my interview, which became the impetus and inspiration for this book.

To further ensure I accurately remembered as much as I possibly could, I subjected several friends to hours of listening to me tell the same stories as I walked them through my photographs, taking notes then or immediately afterward to make sure I was remembering the same things the same way, as well as spending hours on the phone doing the same thing (again, *read*: monologues) with my dear friend and editor, Beth— conversations we also recorded and had transcribed.

Where I could not recall specific facts about a place (for example, the size, or length, or number of objects), I have consulted Wikipedia, Wikitravel, Lonely Planet, the Koryo Tours website, my personal trip itinerary, and in some cases Tripadvisor.com to see if anyone else had the information. This being North Korea, land of subterfuge and misinformation, even things as simple as the names of buildings and Great Leaders are inconsistent, so I just chose whatever was most common or what I liked best.

I've withheld all names for safety. No joke. Although it probably won't help. This is something I feel very conflicted about. On the one hand, my handlers must know the inherent risks in their jobs. On the other hand, what choice do they have? And I have to believe the Party did some type of vetting before agreeing to let me in. I may not be a journalist or professional photographer, but my words and photographs are all over the internet, and it's not hard to see that I pull no punches. Nevertheless I have a very heavy heart when it comes to Older Handler, Fresh Handler, Driver, and the others, and I sincerely wish them (really, truly hope for) no harm.

I wrestled with whether I was qualified to write a book—or do a podcast, for that matter—about North Korea. After all, I was just a tourist who'd visited the country for ten days. But most people visit North Korea for three to five nights on a pre-arranged group tour, accompanied by a Western tour leader in addition to the North Korean guides, who accompany the group for the duration of their stay. Far fewer do what I did and go for longer, independently, on a fully customized tour, with no Western guide, accompanied only by North Korean guides (handlers) assigned to them by the KITC. This I believe gave me a far richer, more in-depth experience.

More importantly, in the end, this isn't a book about North Korea—not in an academic or reportage sense, anyway. It's a book about me being in North Korea and what my experience was like there. I lay no claims to being an expert or even right about what I saw in North Korea. All I know is what I saw, and in North Korea, seeing is *not* believing.

Here's what I do know:

1. I have great instincts, high emotional intelligence, and a tremendous amount of empathy.

2. I tend to get what's going on, even when no one else around me does.

3. I have been all over the world—really traveled and explored it—and I've learned that the more you travel, the more patterns you recognize.

4. Nine nights and ten days in North Korea is a relatively long amount of time, and I was not free to just *be* on this trip. I was never alone.

I was on a structured, hour-by-hour tour, up early every day and dragged around for twelve to fourteen hours, from site to site, activity to activity. And I was lectured at throughout. My only breaks were when occasionally I was able to dine alone and when I was in my room sleeping. There was no going with the flow. No stopping in cafes to soak it all in. No "I think I'll skip that and sleep in" days. It's a sprint, and a marathon. So all in, I believe I saw a lot.

5. I was with the same handlers the entire time. We never left each other's sides. There were no shifts, no other tourists in our group to take the pressure off me or them. Just us. And people are people: after a while, you forget to keep your guard up all the time. Shit happens. They made mistakes. Said things they shouldn't have said. Let me see things they probably shouldn't have. Contradicted themselves. Let their emotions get the best of them. Were lazy. Were human. If you pay attention, you learn a lot.

6. I asked a ton of questions, and I was relentless about it. I am tenacious and determined when something makes no sense. Ask a question many different ways, over the course of several different days, and you can tease out information.

7. On the other hand, I often stopped talking altogether. Initially this was because I would be frustrated and worried that I'd push too far and say something that might cause trouble for me or for them. But it turned out that, as well prepared as my handlers were for questions, they were totally unprepared for silence. In the absence of asking questions, or me speaking, they simply over-talked.

8. We were not confined to Pyongyang, North Korea's "gleaming" capital city, meant to showcase the country's wealth, abundance,

and progress. The government does its level best to control everything inside of Pyongyang (and even then it fails), but cross the city line, as I did several times, and it's Third World 101. Small cities and towns and the rural areas between them are primitive and run-down at best. Not even the Wizard of Oz could hide that. And spend enough time inside Pyongyang, and you see that all is not so shiny and new. I didn't have to look hard to find the city's cracks. I just had to look.

9. I've been managing people my entire career. I know when people are lying to me.

10. Everybody lies.

HERE ONE OF THE GUINEA-PIGS CHEERED, AND WAS IMMEDIATELY SUPPRESSED BY THE OFFICERS OF THE COURT.

LEWIS CARROLL

Alice's Adventures in Wonderland

THE "SHIT I THINK MIGHT BE REAL" LIST

In no particular order—except for the bride, who started it all:

1. The bride's unmistakable stink eye at the wedding reception I crashed.

2. The wedding reception I crashed.

3. Driver and I giving each other shit at meals for smoking and being vegetarian. And me hurting his feelings.

4. The guard who was out of uniform, and asleep, when we arrived at the Paeksong Food Factory.

5. Of the two workers I saw at the Paeksong Food Factory, the one who gave me the stink eye.

6. The little boy who was brave enough to break rank from his friends, risking ridicule and social suicide to stand in the same subway car with me, but who then caved seconds later and fled the train.

7. The people on the subway who spontaneously laughed when an old woman and I both made a move at the same time and caused

a millisecond of confusion. Normally, cause for DISCUSSIONS on the NoKo propaganda tour…not unmitigated joy.

8. When Fresh Handler shrieked and squealed at the football match, and I taught her to talk smack.

9. When Older Handler screamed "dammit" at the football match.

10. When Fresh Handler giggled as Local Handler tried to explain that the Earth rotates around the Sun.

11. My moment of utter clarity in the hot-not spa.

12. While we were driving inside the DMZ, the look of disbelief on Older Handler's face when I asked if they would pull the car over to shoo a bug out of it.

13. The fact that I thought Non-General, our local guide at the DMZ, was cute, so I tried to fix Fresh Handler up with him because she'd told me her parents were pressuring her to get married. Older Handler intervened, letting us know that Non-General was (unfortunately, sadly) married, but not before Fresh Handler agreed he was cute.

14. Really, any expression on Older Handler's face that was not a smile: e.g., when she showed flashes of annoyance, aggravation, or frustration. And Older Handler's attitude on Day One when I didn't want to try special North Korean orange ice-cream treat.

15. After telling Older Handler I felt like I was in prison at the Koryo Hotel because there was no place to sit outside, anytime we went

anyplace with an acceptable spot for me to sit outside, she would point to it and snidely say, "You sit there since you feel like you are in prison."

16. When we were picnicking at Dragon Mountain inside the Sariwon Folk Village, we encountered a huge group of young schoolchildren, too young to be Young Pioneers. They had seen me walk to the top of the hill and I guess begged their teachers to let them wait for me to come back down. Older Handler knew I loved photographing kids, and for once she seemed excited to let me know of this imminent score. When we got to the bottom of the hill, the kids went certifiably mental—they were so thrilled! Dozens and dozens and dozens of them surrounded and followed me, ceaselessly shouting, "Hell-oh! Good-bye!" over and over again as they waved. The children's authentic joy was matched by Fresh Handler's sheer surprise and delight. "I never see anything like that before," she said, while Older Handler pretended she hadn't noticed—her frozen countenance reflecting her abject lack of emotion.

17. Right after my child fans mobbed me, we walked to the bottom of Dragon Mountain, near the entrance of the Sariwon Folk Village. To the right of the entrance were nine or ten giant panels, all in a row, that told the "history" of North Korea (*read*: propaganda about the American Imperialists and our atrocities). It was the middle of the afternoon and about a thousand degrees outside. I was lethargic, and I had to pee. And I'd seen this dog-and-pony show a few times by now and could seriously not care less. So I said to Older Handler, in sort of a teasing (but serious) way, "I get it. I get it. American Imperialist atrocities this, thirteenth-century atrocities that. Can we please skip ahead? I've got to pee." Before she could

catch herself, Fresh Handler spontaneously giggled but shut right down when Older Handler gave her a major stink eye.

18. Fresh Handler and I got our periods the same day. We bonded over cramps. Now THAT shit was real.

19. The smile that broke across Non-General's face as he watched his image come together from the blank piece of instant film.

20. When sweet Boyfriend General called me brave for visiting North Korea.

ACKNOWLEDGMENTS

I want to thank Older Handler, Fresh Handler, and Driver for an experience I will never forget—one that truly changed my life—and Simon Cockerell of Koryo Group for organizing my trip. Without these four people, I would have no story to share.

To Beth Price, my coach, teacher, editor, researcher, sounding board, problem solver, therapist, cheerleader, and friend for over twenty years, who was by my side from the moment I typed the first word on the page. Without her tireless support and input every single step of the way, this book would not have seen the light of day.

To Christine Moore and Linda Schmidt, my editors, whose invaluable expertise, spot on advice, thoughtfulness, and enthusiasm cannot be overstated. And to Laura Kopp, my proofreader, for finding mistakes I would have bet my house didn't exist...proving unequivocally why you need a great proofreader.

To Erin Tyler, my book designer—inside and out—for transforming simple words on a page into such a beautiful (and real!) book. Unlike the Dear Great Leaders, her "on-the-spot guidance" really did make magic happen.

To James Altucher. Being interviewed by him on North Korea for his podcast became the impetus for this book, and professional contacts he so generously shared with me became part of the team who were central to the development of my book.

To my sister, Kristy Simmons, for her love and encouragement, keen insight, and great feedback. I love and adore her to pieces.

To Fabrizio LaRocca, my photo editor, website designer, and overall giver of awesome advice. His dedication, patience and care are rare in this day and age.

To Peter Clark for doing the impossible...knowing how to actually publish this book. Were it not for Peter, I would be selling this book from a lemonade stand, and I would have printed it at Kinkos (no offense to Kinkos).

To Rachel Blishe, Yujin Kim, and Jennifer Arnow for their incredible work on my personal website (wendysimmons.com), and to the talented team at Filtro for building an awesome website for this book (MyHolidayIn-NorthKorea.com) in no time at all (and with no power tools!).

To my mom and Michael for loving me unconditionally, and always letting me know it. It's everything. I love you both very much.

And to all my friends who have encouraged my writing, and this book, and have always been there when I've needed them. I am incredibly lucky to be surrounded by so many kind and nurturing people.

All quotes are from The Project Gutenberg eBook editions of Lewis Carroll's *Alice's Adventures in Wonderland and Through the Looking-Glass.*

ABOUT THE AUTHOR

Wendy Simmons won't stop travelling until she visits every country in the world! Despite her hatred for packing, she's managed to explore more than eighty-five so far—including territories and colonies—and chronicles her adventures on her blog, wendysimmons.com.

She is president of Vendeloo, a consultancy she founded in 2001, Chief Brand Officer of a NYC-based global eyewear brand, and an award-winning photographer. She's also owned a bar in Manhattan, worked for a lobbying firm on Capitol Hill, and written a Japanese-language phrase book. Though her Japanese is now terrible, Wendy's Pig Latin is flourishing. She graduated summa cum laude and Phi Beta Kappa from George Washington University.

Wendy practices Muay Thai daily and lives in Brooklyn in a converted 1800s schoolhouse.

Full-size versions of all photographs featured in *My Holiday in North Korea: The Funniest Worst Place on Earth* can be viewed at MyHolidayInNorthKorea.com. Additional photos from North Korea can be viewed on her blog.